THE PUFFIN BOOK OF
100 GREAT INDIANS

READ MORE IN PUFFIN

The Puffin Book of 100 Extraordinary Indians

THE PUFFIN
BOOK OF

100

great

INDIANS

Illustrations by KALLOL MAJUMDER

PUFFIN BOOKS
An imprint of Penguin Random House

PUFFIN BOOKS

USA | Canada | UK | Ireland | Australia
New Zealand | India | South Africa | China

Puffin Books is part of the Penguin Random House group of companies
whose addresses can be found at global.penguinrandomhouse.com

Published by Penguin Random House India Pvt. Ltd
4th Floor, Capital Tower 1, MG Road,
Gurugram 122 002, Haryana, India

Penguin
Random House
India

First published in Puffin by Penguin Books India 2012
This edition published in Puffin Books by Penguin Random House India 2022

Text and illustrations copyright © Penguin Books India 2012
Content researched and developed by excalibEr Solutions

ISBN 9780143331735

Typeset in Sabon by InoSoft Systems, Noida
Printed at Replika Press Pvt. Ltd, India

www.penguin.co.in

Contents

Mr Perfectionist

Name: Aamir Hussain Khan
Birth Date: 14 March 1965
Place: Bombay (now Mumbai), Maharashtra

Very few aspiring actors, who have a golden platter of offers laid in front of them backed by their lineage, manage to exploit the situation and carve a niche for themselves. However, the story of this actor, who has established his own identity through sheer hard work and talent, is quite unique.

Aamir Khan never really had to struggle to gain a foothold in the Hindi film industry. He had a brief stint in the movies as a child actor in *Yaadon Ki Baaraat*, followed by a small role in *Madhoshi*. He then went on to play national-level tennis for Maharashtra. Eleven years later, he made a comeback in *Holi* but it was in the blockbuster *Qayamat Se Qayamat Tak* that he stole the limelight. Overnight, chocolate boy Aamir became the nation's heart-throb.

After his first commercial success, Aamir signed on quite a number of films that, unfortunately, did not earn great acclaim. His acting talent was noticed though, and he became one of the ruling Khans of Bollywood. He won the best male debut award in 1989 for *Qayamat Se Qayamat Tak* and received the Filmfare Best Actor Award in 1996 for *Raja Hindustani*.

Aamir's next big breakthrough came in 2001 when he produced and played the lead role in *Lagaan*. Apart from being commercially successful and winning seven National Film Awards, *Lagaan* was also nominated in the Best Foreign Language Film category at the Academy Awards. However, in the same year, Aamir's fifteen-year-old marriage to Reena Dutta ended and she retained custody of their two children, Junaid and Ira.

Aamir took a break for the next four years. In 2005, he made a comeback with *Mangal Pandey: The Rising*. The film was fraught with controversies and did not fare as expected at the box office. In the same year, Aamir married Kiran Rao, also a film-maker. Kiran later wrote the script of and directed the film *Dhobi Ghat*, starring Aamir.

At this point in his career, Aamir took a stand that no other major Bollywood star had ever done. He decided to do just one film at a time and get completely involved in the process of film-making. He also insisted on reading a completed script before signing a project. Such dedication towards his profession earned him the title of 'Mr Perfectionist'.

Aamir has often been criticized in the media for interfering in the process of film production but he has remained undaunted. He has followed his heart and made his producers happy by delivering one phenomenal hit after the other. Some of his successes are *Rang de Basanti* [2005] and *Fanaa* [2006]. A descendant of Muslim scholar–politician Maulana Abul Kalam Azad, Aamir made his directorial debut with *Taare Zameen Par*, which won critical and commercial acclaim. Aamir also delivered marvellous performances in *Ghajini* and *3 Idiots* and shattered many box office records in the history of Indian cinema. He is currently one of the highest paid actors in the Hindi film industry.

Aamir has established his versatility by portraying roles across genres like romance, comedy, action and drama. He has also written screenplays and done playback singing. Considered 'a complete actor', he does not get affected by industry rankings. Aamir has also gone on record saying that he does not trust the transparency and credibility of some of the popular cinematic awards. As a matter of fact, he makes it a point not to attend many of the star-studded award functions. He also turned down the proposal to have his wax statue installed at Madame Tussauds in London.

Aamir's acting brilliance has earned him the prestigious Padma Shri and Padma Bhushan awards. Though he has been in the industry for over two decades, his performances are always refreshing. He has become such a seasoned artist over time that people flock to the theatres enticed by the enigma of his name.

Gold Finger

Name: Abhinav Bindra
Birth Date: 28 September 1982
Place: Dehradun, Uttarakhand

Abhinav Bindra was the youngest Indian participant in the 2000 Sydney Olympic Games. Although he could not qualify for the finals, this exposure was a stepping stone for the young shooter who made a powerful comeback in the 2008 Beijing Olympic Games. By winning the 10 m air rifle shooting competition, he became the first Indian ever to win an Olympic gold medal for an individual event.

However, success did not come easy for this calm and composed professional. Abhinav was aware of the highs and lows of winning and losing in sports from a very young age. His eventful journey in shooting was rife with ups and downs and he understood how to face testing times early on. In 1998, at the age of fifteen, he participated in the Commonwealth Games. He won his first laurels, a bronze medal, at the Munich World Cup in 2001. However, his performance in the 2004 Athens Olympic Games was disappointing and he missed the

2006 Asian Games due to a back injury. He continued training and, in 2006 itself, became the first Indian shooter to win a World Championship gold in Zagreb.

Abhinav displayed an interest in sports right from childhood. When he began his shooting journey in his teens, his parents supported his passion and installed an indoor shooting range at their home to help him focus and practise. Unfortunately, his young body could not withstand the strain of rigorous sessions. He suffered and battled back pain and a muscular problem that threatened to end his shooting career. Yet, he kept his fears at bay and dreamt of participating in the Olympics. He focused on rehabilitation through exercise and therapy to regain his original form. He took formal training for shooting in Germany. The next challenge was to organize funds to participate in international events. This was not an easy task as the sport was still not popular or recognized in India.

After almost thirteen years of patience, dedication, hard work, focus, concentration, rigorous practice, and, of course, the never-ending hope that he carried in his heart, Abhinav tasted glorious victory when he gracefully bowed to receive his gold medal at the 2008 Beijing Olympics while the national anthem was being played.

His memorable feat of winning the gold was arguably one of the biggest achievements in the history of Indian sports. Every newspaper in India described the magical moment and publicized Abhinav's triumph. He received awards from various state governments and other private organizations. However, success did not go to his head. He resolved to go all out to do whatever it took to improve his future performances and increase the popularity of this sport.

Abhinav was the youngest Indian to be awarded the Rajiv Gandhi Khel Ratna award at the age of nineteen for his valuable contribution to the sport of shooting. He is undisputedly one of the brightest stars in the current generation of shooters and has surprised both national and international audiences with his career graph.

Abhinav still practises between twelve to fourteen hours every day. Since shooting is mentally strenuous, he has a coach to hone his mental faculties as well. At the 2010 Commonwealth Games held in New Delhi, Abhinav was given the honour of being the flag-bearer of the Indian contingent at the opening ceremony. He also took the athletes' oath on behalf of participants from all countries.

Abhinav has enjoyed a glorious academic and professional stint as well. This successful entrepreneur floated two companies after completing his Bachelors and Masters degrees in business administration.

He has also set up the Abhinav Bindra Foundation, which strives to provide access to various amenities like education, health care and sports to the lesser privileged people. Apart from vocational training, the foundation also trains and supports sports enthusiasts who aspire to participate in the Olympics.

Angel of Mercy

Name: Agnes Gonxha Bojaxhiu
Birth Date: 26 August 1910
Place: Üsküb, Ottoman Empire (now Skopje, Macedonia)
Death Date: 5 September 1997
Place: Calcutta, West Bengal

The Missionaries of Charity is a group of very motivated nuns devoted to the service of the poorest of the world's poor. In their early days, as the congregation of sisters grew, their quarters became too cramped for accommodation. So they moved into a new home in Calcutta in 1953. The new surroundings were spacious but the nuns of the order lived a life shaped by extreme poverty. They fulfilled only their basic needs but denied themselves even a hint of luxury. Their founder explained: 'In order to understand and help those who have nothing, we must live like them. . . The only difference is they are poor by birth, we are poor by choice.' Such was the empathy and dedication Mother Teresa had for the people she served.

Born Agnes Gonxha Bojaxhiu in faraway Macedonia over a century ago, she acknowledged, from the tender age of twelve, the call of God that she had to be a missionary to spread the love of Christ.

Agnes was fascinated by stories of the lives of missionaries and their service in Bengal, and was convinced that she should commit herself to a religious life. At the age of eighteen, she left her parental home and joined Sisters of Loreto, an Irish community of nuns with missions in India. At twenty-one, she took her vows as a nun and joined the convent. However, the suffering and poverty outside the walls of the convent impacted her so deeply that after serving in the convent for two decades, she devoted herself to working in the slums of Calcutta.

Agnes had sought and procured Indian citizenship to settle and live among the people she had committed her life to. On 7 October 1950, she received permission from the Vatican to start her own order, the Missionaries of Charity, whose primary task was to love and care for those people whom nobody else was prepared to look after.

Her compassion was extraordinary. She didn't think twice before touching a leper on the road or cleaning a festering wound on an unfortunate soul. She did not hesitate to eat with the poor even though she had gone on to share the stage with world leaders. Social workers all around the world drew inspiration from her work and commitment to her cause.

She would often say, 'I don't do all this for charity. I do it for Christ.' For her, the poor were not like

Christ—they were Christ. Critics condemned her, saying she did what she did in an effort to convert people to the Catholic faith. She would hear them out and then say, 'I am an Indian, India is mine.' She always urged Hindus to be better Hindus, Muslims to be better Muslims and Parsis to be better Parsis. In her task of serving the community, she believed in the importance of communication and could speak fluently in English, Albanian, Serbo-Croat, Bengali, and Hindi.

Today, the missionaries of her order are spread all over the world, including the former Soviet Union and other eastern European countries. They help the poor in the Asia, Africa, and Latin America, and also undertake relief work during natural catastrophes such as floods, epidemics, and famines. The order tends to alcoholics, the homeless, and those suffering from AIDS. The order that started with twelve members in Calcutta has over 4,000 nuns now.

Mother Teresa's work has been recognized and acclaimed across the world. She received a number of awards and distinctions, including the Pope John XXIII Peace Prize in 1971 and the Nehru Prize in 1972 for promoting international peace and understanding. She also received the Balzan Prize in 1979 and the Templeton and Magsaysay awards, apart from the prestigious Nobel Peace Prize in 1979 and the Bharat Ratna in 1980.

On 13 March 1997, Mother Teresa stepped down as the head of Missionaries of Charity. She passed away on 5 September in the same year, just days after she turned eighty-seven. In 2003, she was beatified by Pope John Paul II and called 'Blessed Teresa of Calcutta'.

On 28 Aug 2010, to commemorate the centenary of her birth, the Government of India issued a special 5-rupee coin.

The Missionaries' white sari with a blue border symbolizes compassion even after the Angel of Mercy has departed. It is a beacon of hope to the suffering millions across the world.

The Greatest Mughal Emperor

Name: Akbar
Birth Date: 15 October 1542
Place: Umerkot, Sindh (now in Pakistan)
Death Date: 27 October 1605
Place: Fatehpur Sikri, Agra

Akbar was once crossing a forest in central India with his royal entourage when a tigress sprang at them. Akbar was only nineteen at the time but while his men froze with terror on seeing the beast, he remained unfazed and struck instantly, killing the tigress with one blow of his sword.

This is just one of the many anecdotes about Akbar's legendary courage, which has been chronicled in *Akbarnama* ('Book of Akbar') written in Persian by his court historian and biographer Abul Fazl.

Jalaluddin Muhammad Akbar, or Akbar the Great as he is commonly known, is widely considered to be the greatest Mughal emperor. His grandfather Babur founded the Mughal dynasty in India. His father Humayun died when Akbar was just thirteen, leaving him in the care of a very competent statesman and warrior, Bairam Khan. Acting as regent, Bairam Khan managed the empire on Akbar's behalf for the next five years. He also inculcated in Akbar all the skills necessary to become an able administrator and warrior.

On his part, Akbar showed immense aptitude for feats that required strength, agility, and presence of mind. He proved to be excellent at swordsmanship, combat, hunting and sports. He was also very good at taming and training wild animals, like elephants and cheetahs.

Akbar was never taught how to read or write. He stayed illiterate all his life. However, he had great love for literature and a tremendous thirst for knowledge. He used to get people to read books to him. The young prince grew up to be a man of refined taste and impressive intellect, well aware of various subjects and matters of the world.

When Akbar turned eighteen, he decided to emerge from Bairam Khan's shadow and rule the empire on his own. Bairam Khan rebelled but was pardoned and treated with respect by Akbar, who never forgot the role that his mentor had played in his early life.

There are records of several instances where Akbar treated offenders ruthlessly, especially those who committed offences repeatedly, but then there are also other instances where he was magnanimous to a fault.

Akbar was a man of many virtues. He propagated a secular outlook and was himself tolerant towards religions other than his own. Akbar's courtiers and generals comprised people from diverse religious backgrounds. He even founded a religion called Din-i-Ilahi, blending the positive aspects of several religions such as Islam, Hinduism, Christianity, and Jainism.

Akbar was a great patron of art and culture. The *navratnas* or 'nine gems' of his court comprised individuals accomplished in music, poetry and writing. His minister Birbal was renowned for his wisdom and wit. Akbar was also instrumental in building the city of Fatehpur Sikri. Situated near Agra, it is today a popular tourist attraction and holds a mirror to Akbar's life and times.

Akbar was an able administrator. He devised a system of taxation that was people-friendly and fair to all. During his reign, he fought off threats and attacks from other kings, using not only force but also tact. He was clever in his diplomatic dealings, and is known to have married the daughters of Rajput kings in order to pre-empt possible threats to his empire.

By the end of Akbar's reign, the Mughal empire encompassed almost the whole of northern and central India. Akbar's multifaceted and awe-inspiring persona has made him an enduring name in Indian history and culture.

The 'Argumentative' Economist

Name: Amartya Sen
Birth Date: 3 November 1933
Place: Santiniketan, West Bengal

Amartya Sen spent some of his early childhood years in Dhaka, Bangladesh. During that time, he witnessed an incident that was to have a deep impact on him. One afternoon, a Muslim daily labourer came running in through the gate of the Sens' house. The man was bleeding profusely. He had come to find work in the neighbourhood, a Hindu-dominated area. He claimed that his wife had cautioned him about going there as communal riots were raging in the city. He had not heeded her warning since he needed to work to earn money, so that his family could eat that day. Just as his wife had feared, the labourer was stabbed by communal rioters. He died in hospital.

This incident stayed in Sen's mind for long after, and got him thinking about issues like identity and poverty. He realized the importance of economic well-being and stability in a person's life. Without them, a person becomes a pawn in the hands of others, just like the unfortunate labourer. Had the labourer possessed adequate income, he and his family could have managed their meal for the day without him having to hazard his life.

Much later in his life, Sen went on to win the Nobel Prize for Economics, for his work in the area of welfare economics. Welfare economics dwells on the subject of the economic well-being of the people. It deals with social welfare measured in terms of economic welfare of individuals.

Sen became known for his concern for the poorer sections of society. He received recognition for his extensive work specifically regarding the subject of famines, and ways and means of alleviating the hardships caused by famines. This could have had something to do with the fact that he was witness to the Bengal famine of 1943, in which millions of people, mostly landless rural labourers, had died.

Sen's scholarly pursuits are not surprising considering the family he comes from. Sen's father was a professor of chemistry at Dhaka University. His grandfather was a teacher and scholar who worked extensively with Rabindranath Tagore. Much of Sen's education was at Tagore's school in Santiniketan.

After his stint at Santiniketan, Sen studied at Presidency College in Kolkata and then at Trinity College in Cambridge. He went on to teach at prestigious institutions and universities such as Delhi School of Economics, London School of Economics, Oxford University and Harvard University. He has also taught as a visiting faculty at various other universities.

Sen has been honoured with the Bharat Ratna by the Indian government. He has also been referred to as 'the Conscience and the Mother Teresa of Economics' for his work involving the poorer sections of society.

Sen continues to visit his childhood home at Santiniketan every year. He also has a home in America. His first marriage to renowned Bengali poet Naboneeta Dev Sen ended in a divorce. He remarried but, unfortunately, his second wife succumbed to cancer. Sen is now married, for the third time, to Emma Rothschild, also an economics scholar.

Sen has written numerous books and essays, which have been translated into several languages. *The Argumentative Indian* and *The Idea of Justice* are two of his well-known books. When he was once asked how he likes to spend his time, he said, 'I read a lot and like arguing with people.' *Time* magazine cited Sen as one of the 100 most influential persons in the world in 2010.

The Angry Young Man of Bollywood

Name: Amitabh Bachchan
Birth Date: 11 October 1942
Place: Allahabad, Uttar Pradesh

For some people, pain dilutes the zeal to face life. But for some evergreen legends, it becomes the fuel to face life's challenges and even enjoy the struggle.

Such is the story of a tall, lean young man who applied to All India Radio for the post of an announcer after quitting his job as a freight broker in Calcutta. Ironically, he was rejected for his deep voice, an attribute that earned him distinction later. This introvert then tried his hand at filmdom and initially faced a series of flops. His unconventional looks were not appreciated by the directors of those times who preferred good-looking, mellow, romantic heroes. He was also advised to soften his voice to suit the industry.

However, in 1973, when a film named *Zanjeer* was released, the world met a new angry young man who was the people's saviour and took the law in his hands. He set a trend and created a permanent niche for himself in the industry. Over the years, he has reminded his critics repeatedly that he is here to stay—for as long as he wills!

Fondly called Big B by his fans, he was originally named Amit Srivatsava and was born to a great poet, Harivansh Rai Bachchan, and Teji Bachchan. He is none other than Amitabh Bachchan, the noted film actor and a prominent TV personality. This multitalented actor is the husband of Jaya Bhaduri, an accomplished actress in her own right; the proud father of Abhishek Bachchan, a new generation actor of Hindi cinema; and a doting father-in-law to Aishwarya Rai Bachchan, former Miss World and a well-known film star.

True to his name, which means 'brilliance unlimited', Amitabh has shown unmatched professional brilliance. With numerous awards in his kitty, including four National Awards and fourteen Filmfare Awards, he still challenges the new generation of actors by being one of the busiest actors around. In addition to acting, Bachchan has been a playback singer and rendered his unique voice to some popular songs, such as *Rang barse* and *Mere angane mein*, and also to poetry renditions.

In year 1982, a near-fatal accident on the sets of the film *Coolie* forced Amitabh to take a break from films. He then briefly ventured into politics. His close association with former prime ministers Indira Gandhi and Rajiv Gandhi is well known. He also served as a Member of Parliament for three years from 1984 to

1987 but then resigned and decided never to return to politics.

Amitabh made a comeback in films in 1988 with *Shahenshah*. However, this was followed by a series of flops. During the mid 1990s, he pioneered an ambitious company named Amitabh Bachchan Corporation Ltd (ABCL). The first few films produced by the company failed. When the Miss World beauty pageant event held in Bangalore in 1996 was mismanaged, the company collapsed, plunging the Bachchan empire into bankruptcy.

Critics wrote him off as a failure. However, Amitabh proved them all wrong in 2000 when he rose like a phoenix in the popular TV show *Kaun Banega Crorepati*. The first season of this game show enjoyed huge success across India, as it captured the attention of almost every household and challenged cinema hall occupancy.

Bachchan again returned to filmdom and delivered films such as *Black*, *Khakee* and *Nishabd*. The movies enjoyed varying degrees of commercial success. Amitabh won accolades for almost all his roles, so much so that his fans never stopped asking for more.

Pushing seventy now, Amitabh Bachchan is still considered a priceless icon of India's film and media. He was the first Indian actor whose wax statue was showcased in Madame Tussauds in London.

Sarod Samrat

Name: Amjad Ali Khan
Birth Date: 9 October 1945
Place: Gwalior, Madhya Pradesh

He is a sixth-generation musician of the Bangash lineage. He has created magic with his favourite musical instrument, the sarod, which he has simplified to play complex notes with ease, spanning three octaves just by using his fingernails.

Masoom Ali Khan was homeschooled and spent his formative years enjoying the musical tutelage of his reputed father, Haafiz Ali Khan. At the tender age of six, he started performing in concerts. He was later rechristened Amjad Ali Khan by a sage.

Khan gave his solo debut recital when he was just twelve. His career graph skyrocketed in the 1960s when he started performing at many reputed international festivals. Khan's innovative musical compositions and elegant style earned him national and global fame.

Khan believes in gracefully blending love and music, the two predominant forces that drive his life. His brilliance was noticed worldwide when he added his interpretation and created new ragas in music like Kamalashree and Priyadarshini. His melodious compositions include *Haripriya Kanada*, *Kiran Ranjani*, *Shivanjali*, *Bapukauns* and *Lalit Dhwani*.

He was the first North Indian musician to perform at the reputed Thiruvaiyuru Music Festival in honour of Thyagaraja. He has also performed many times at various international venues like Royal Albert Hall, Carnegie Hall, Mozart Hall and Opera House. Some of his notable compositions include *Tribute to Hong Kong*, a masterpiece in collaboration with reputed instrumentalists; his signature tune for the 48th International Film Festival and also *Bhairav*, one of his best albums that was ranked among the top fifty classical albums of the world. Some of his prestigious performances were at the World Arts Summit in Venice, at the Central Hall of the Indian Parliament to commemorate sixty years of Indian Independence and also at the UN peace concert during the ninth anniversary of the 9/11 tragedy.

In 1976, Khan married Subhalakshmi, an acclaimed Bharatanatyam dancer who gave up her illustrious career to take care of the family. Their sons, Amaan and Ayaan, are promising sarod players who carry forth their father's legacy and family lineage.

Ustad Amjad Ali Khan's ancestral home has been converted into 'Sarod Ghar', a musical museum with a rich display of instruments. The Ustad Hafiz Ali Khan Memorial Society was started in 1997 in memory of his father and guru. This society recognizes eminent artists and organizes music festivals annually. Khan has also trained many other sarodiyas. He emphasizes on preserving classical music by training young children.

Khan is the proud recipient of many honours like Padma Shri, Padma Bhushan, Padma Vibhushan as well as the Crystal Award, UNICEF's National Ambassadorship, UNESCO Award, Sangeet Natak Akademi Award and Fukuoka Asian Culture Prize. The French government has honoured him as Commander of the Order of Arts and letters. The US state of Massachusetts declared 20 April as Amjad Ali Khan Day. He was also nominated for a Grammy award in the best traditional world music category.

A documentary on Amjad Ali Khan, titled *Strings for Freedom*, won the Bengal Film Journalist Association Award. Two books titled *The World of Amjad Ali Khan* and *Abba: God's Greatest Gift To Us* (by his sons) have been written about him. Khan is also associated with the universities of New Mexico, Washington and Yorkshire as a visiting professor.

This musical maestro is a man of integrity both on and off stage. He is active in various philanthropic activities and associated with organizations like Indian Cancer Society, Spastics Society, and various associations for the blind.

Khan's stage presence, refreshing performances, artistry and a gifted aesthetic sense have not withered even after four decades. He has raised the recognition of the sarod, bringing it at par with the sitar.

The Missile Man

Name: A.P.J. Abdul Kalam
Birth Date: 15 October 1931
Place: Rameshwaram, Tamil Nadu

A loyal team of scientists was working on a complicated rocket launch project at Thumba. The scientists were very happy to work on this project. Wonder why? Their boss was an exceptional human being who knew how to treat people with courtesy, concern and care.

The long working hours of the scientists made their lives tedious and stressful. During one such challenging day, a hard-working scientist asked for permission to leave early as he wanted to take his children to an exhibition. The leave was approved and the scientist was determined to complete his allotted work on time. However, the hours flew and by the time he remembered, it was late night. Filled with guilt, he trudged back home, expecting his children to be crying in disappointment and also dreading to face his upset wife.

The scientist was in for a surprise. His wife was pretty relaxed and was reading a newspaper! His children were peacefully asleep. Softly, he asked, 'Were they disappointed about the exhibition?' It was the wife's turn to be amazed. She said, 'Your boss came in the evening and took the children to the exhibition. He said you were busy at work. The children came back tired and slept off.'

This exceptional boss was none other than the former Indian president, Dr Avul Pakir Jainulabdeen Abdul Kalam!

- He is called the 'Missile Man of India'.
- He was India's 11th president, popularly known as the 'People's President'.
- A visionary, he wants to transform India into a developed nation by 2020.

Dr Kalam's success did not come easy to him. Hard work, sincerity, discipline and perseverance transformed his struggles into an inspirational story, incredible yet true. His father was a boat owner who rented his boats to the local fishermen to run his family. To earn an additional income and to support his studies, the young Kalam started his career as a newspaper vendor. During this time, he also began writing inspirational poetry in Tamil and learnt how to play the veena.

This gifted engineer graduated with a science degree from St Joseph's College, Tiruchirappalli, went on to specialize in aeronautical engineering and completed his diploma from Madras Institute of Technology. He contributed to the development of SLV-III, the satellite launch vehicle that won India a membership in the Space Club.

Dr Kalam's motivational speeches are quite popular worldwide. An avid reader of *Thirukkural*, the collection of aphoristic Tamil couplets, he often quotes these in his speeches. He has been instrumental in igniting the minds of youngsters by the power his vision.

In spite of his success and fame, Dr Kalam remains a simple and humble man. Besides being a bachelor, he is a strict vegetarian and an absolute teetotaller.

A disciplinarian who leads his life constructively on his own terms, the living legend has won honorary doctorates from thirty institutions and universities. He is the recipient of several prestigious honours like the Bharat Ratna, Padma Vibhushan, and Padma Bhushan. Dr Kalam has also been awarded the Hoover Medal, America's top engineering award.

Dr Kalam became the first scientist to occupy the Rashtrapati Bhavan. He has always stressed that a country like India should be more assertive in establishing its stand on international relations. To secure a place for India as a superpower in the future, he has contributed a lot to the nuclear weapons programme.

Dr Kalam's literary talent can be noted in his poems, essays, speeches and autobiographies. He has published various popular books that include *Ignited Minds: Unleashing the Power within India*, *India*

2020: A Vision for the New Millennium, and *Wings of Fire*. Besides, he has also written poems on several subjects.

Dr Kalam's philosophy of life can perhaps be summed up in his own words: 'You have to dream before your dreams can come true.'

The Mozart of Madras

Name: A.R. Rahman
Birth Date: 6 January 1966
Place: Madras (now Chennai), Tamil Nadu

Many inspirational stories from around the world have taught us that every struggle provides an opportunity to learn and to progress. Winners never succumb to challenges; they use them as prospects to prove their worth to this world. Such is the story of living legend A.S. Dileep Kumar.

Dileep's life reached a major turning point when he was just nine years old and his father, a music composer and conductor, died of a mysterious illness. While many other children of his age enjoyed their childhood and got a good education, he had to begin supporting his mother and three sisters. The only way to eke out a family income was to rent out his father's musical equipment. Finally, he dropped out of school.

Following in his father's footsteps and encouraged by his mother, Dileep learnt how to play the keyboard, guitar, piano, harmonium and synthesizer. He felt that he could create good music by combining the Eastern classical heritage with the latest Western technologies. When Dileep was eleven, he joined musical troupes and went on world tours as a keyboard player. Eventually, he earned a scholarship from the renowned Trinity College of Music and graduated with a degree in Western classical music.

Tragedy loomed over the family again in the late 1980s, when one of Dileep's sisters fell seriously ill. Having almost lost all hope of her recovery, the family appealed to a pir for help. The girl revived. In 1989, influenced by the pir's teachings, the entire family converted to Islam. Dileep was given a new name that was to take the world by storm, the name that would create history, break several music records and take Indian music to an international level. A legend was born—his name was Allah Rakha Rahman. The world today knows him as A.R. Rahman.

During the early 1990s, Rahman set up his own studio, Panchathan Record Inn, in his backyard and started composing jingles. Mani Ratnam, director of several popular Tamil movies, was looking for a new music director for his upcoming project *Roja*. After some hesitation, Rahman took up the assignment. The film's music was a resounding success. The rest, as they say, is history. Rahman was hailed as a phenomenon and flooded with offers.

Initially, Tamil music was popular only among south Indian audiences. Rahman broke many conventions as he created music that crossed barriers of geography, age and language! He did not only become a popular composer in Indian cinema but lost no opportunity to work with many music directors at the international level. His albums gained instant success as soon as they hit the stands. From trendy music to traditional melodies, Rahman's music is a treat for almost every listener.

With two Grammy Awards, four National Awards, fifteen Filmfare Awards and a Golden Globe Award, Rahman has proved time and again that his talent is here to stay. *Time* magazine appropriately called him 'The Mozart of Madras'. His diehard fans fondly call him *Isai Puyal*, which literally translates into 'music storm'. The Indian government has awarded him the Padma Bhushan.

In 2009, *Time* magazine listed Rahman among the 100 most influential people in the world. His modest recording studio grew into one of the most sophisticated studios in Asia, the Panchathan Record Inn & AM Studios at Kodambakkam, Chennai. He has also set up a conservatory to train aspiring musicians and is deeply committed to humanitarian work.

Rahman has truly proved to the world that music is a universal language and needs no translation or interpretation.

The Unconventional Activist

Name: Aruna Roy
Birth Date: 26 May 1946
Place: Madras, Tamil Nadu

'Unorthodox' is probably the best way to describe this dynamic woman, considering the choices she has made in her life. Her lineage gives us an insight into what inspired her to be so different. Her maternal grandparents married across castes, thus transcending the tradition of the caste system prevalent in the conservative society of those times. Her grandmother was an ardent and fearless social worker. Her grandfather authored textbooks and made them available at affordable rates to poor students.

Aruna's family disregarded distinctions of caste and religion and emphasized equal treatment to every human being. Aruna's mother Hema was educated in Christian schools, something almost unheard of in those times. An all-rounder herself, she married only when she turned twenty-five, rather late compared with the standard marital age of Indian women in her era. Aruna's father Elupai Doraiswami Jayaram also hailed from a family of social activists and had participated in the freedom struggle.

Aruna was the couple's eldest child and was trained to be a free thinker from childhood. Her primary education was in a convent. She also learnt classical dance and music at Kalakshetra, the famous arts institution in Chennai.

Aruna's family spoke Hindi and English, apart from their mother tongue Tamil. At her father's insistence, she studied French too. From a very young age, she was a voracious reader of books from all over the world. She shared a great relationship with her parents who encouraged her to share her opinions without inhibitions. Aruna chose to pursue English literature and met her future husband Sanjit 'Bunker' Roy during her post graduation. Bunker also hailed from a progressive family and had raised his voice against the caste system after his sister met her death in a *sati* ceremony.

Aruna was not willing to settle down in a conventional marriage or become a homemaker. She was one of only ten women who qualified in the Civil Services Examination in 1968 and became an IAS officer of the Tamil Nadu cadre. She later got a transfer to the north and came across the harsh realities of being a civil servant. Time and again, she had to fight for her identity—being a woman, she was often not taken seriously as an administrative officer.

Aruna and Bunker were married in 1970 in a simple wedding ceremony. Her marriage was also as unconventional as her other choices. The couple decided not to have children and to give each other a lot of personal space for their individual growth. They also refrained from imposing their beliefs on each other.

Aruna shifted to Delhi to be closer to her husband. As she progressed from one post to the next, the systemic corruption and bureaucratic red tape frustrated her. She realized that the citizens were unaware of their rights and unable to speak for themselves.

Disillusioned and shocked with the system, she quit the service and joined her husband at Tilonia, where he had set up an NGO known as Barefoot College. This was one of the biggest turning points of her life, as she was exposed to the ground realities in rural India.

At Tilonia, Aruna had to adjust to a simple and holistic lifestyle, which was quite a challenge for her after holding positions of such authority. It took her some time to find the knack of interacting with the villagers. She is still thankful to the people there, who transformed her life into a meaningful one by helping her choose the path that would have otherwise been unexplored.

Aruna participated in the work in Tilonia till about 1983, then moved to Devdungri and in association with former colleagues set up the powerful Mazdoor Kisan Shakti Sangathan (MKSS) union for the rights of workers and peasants. The MKSS has no set hierarchy or constitution till today. Many allegations and controversies have been raised about it but the organization has gradually became powerful by attacking corruption at the grass roots, claiming the rights of the citizens to information, and fighting for transparency and accountability of the government.

Between 2004 and 2006, Aruna was a member of the National Advisory Council, where she played a vital role in incorporating the entitlement of citizens into the Right to Information and National Rural Employment Guarantee Acts. She received the Ramon Magsaysay Award in 2000. Her efforts also bore fruit when the Right to Information Act was passed in 2005. Aruna is also a member of the National Employment Guarantee Council.

Aruna is happy that her work thrives on transparency and honesty but thinks that there is still a long way for India to go in order to achieve empowerment and implement the power of democracy.

Booker Winner and Social Activist

Name: Arundhati Roy
Birth Date: 24 November 1961
Place: Shillong, Meghalaya

As a teenager, Arundhati Roy shared a strained relationship with her mother Mary Roy. So much so that she actually left home, or was forced to leave home, when she was just sixteen. It is said that she didn't speak to her mother for six years after that. Yet, years later, she dedicated her debut novel *The God of Small Things* to Mary who, in Arundhati's own words, 'loved me enough to let me go'.

After leaving home in the small town of Ayemenem in Kerala Arundhati led quite an unconventional life, much like her mother who had herself challenged the laws of inheritance and rebelled against many of the social mores of her time. To fend for herself, Arundhati took up odd jobs. She worked as an aerobics instructor briefly, studied architecture in Delhi, wrote screenplays for a couple of films and even acted as a tribal girl in the film *Massey Sahib* before going on to write her first novel.

The God of Small Things shot to fame instantly, not only in India but also overseas. Arundhati became a celebrated novelist almost overnight and went on to win the Booker Prize in 1997 for it. The novel managed to strike an emotional chord in many readers across the world, and much praise was lavished on Arundhati's writing style. The novel is semi-autobiographical. It is set in Ayemenem, where Arundhati herself grew up, and many of its elements resemble her life and that of her family.

If there were people who expected Arundhati to follow up her successful debut novel with many more works of fiction, they were left surprised. She has not written any other novels since *The God of Small Things*. However, she continues to write non-fiction and remains in the public eye by way of her involvement in a number of social causes. Arundhati has raised her voice against many contemporary evils, including the negative impact of rapid globalization and industrialization.

One of the causes that she remains involved with is the Narmada Bachao Andolan, a movement to protest the building of the Sardar Sarovar Dam on the river Narmada in Gujarat. Her essay, 'The Greater Common Good', expressing her views on this project, attracted much attention.

Arundhati has continually voiced her opinions on social and national issues through a number of columns in leading publications, through her collections of essays, The *Algebra of Infinite Justice* and *The Cost of Living*, and through *The Shape of the Beast,* a compilation of interviews that question the notions of democracy, power and justice.

In the recent past, Arundhati has expressed her views on the Kashmir issue, that has major political ramifications in India. Some of her comments implying that Kashmir has 'never been an integral part of India' have been seen as offensive by certain sections. She has even been threatened with arrest for her seditious remarks.

All through, Arundhati's brand of activism has won her bouquets as well as brickbats.

In 1989, Arundhati won the National Film Award for Best Screenplay for her work on the film *In Which Annie Gives It Those Ones*. She is a recipient of Lannan Foundation's Cultural Freedom Award and the Sydney Peace Prize. She was awarded the Sahitya Akademi Award in 2006 for her essays on contemporary issues, but she declined it. In 2011, she received the Norman Mailer Prize for Distinguished Writing.

The Discoverer of Zero

Name: Aryabhata
Birth Date: AD 476
Birth Place: Bihar
Death Date: AD 550

As one of the earliest pioneers of astronomy and mathematics in India, Aryabhata gave a whole new dimension to propositions, rules, formulae, theorems, equations, and widespread beliefs that existed during the golden era of the Gupta reign. He discovered the number 0 or *shunya* and the value of pi ($\varpi = 3.1416$), both of which became vital to mathematical calculations. He exposed the world to stunning astronomical facts thereby disproving the assumptions of those times.

Aryabhata was an innovative thinker well ahead of his time. This genius laid the foundation for the concept of gravity about 1500 years before Galileo and Copernicus propounded it.

There are various stories about Aryabhata's birth and education. However, it is known that he was largely educated at Nalanda University in Pataliputra and contributed exceptional works there, for which he was later made the head of the university.

Unfortunately, many of Aryabhata's works have been lost over time. *Arya-siddhanta* and *Aryabhatiya*, his popular masterpieces, written in the form of verses, contains valuable astronomical and mathematical hypotheses.

As a mathematician, Aryabhata studied various topics such as arithmetic, spherical and plane trigonometry and algebra. He wrote the table of sines, solved quadratic equations, power series equations as well as fractions. He also defined methods to find the square and cube root of a number.

As an astronomer, Aryabhata postulated that the earth is spherical and revolves around the sun. He also explained the rotation of the moon around the earth. He studied the concepts of planetary distances and motions and calculated the earth's circumference. He explained the phenomenon of days and nights, calculated the length of a year and clarified the scientific reason for eclipses. Aryabhata's calculations form the basis of the Jalali calendar as well as the Hindu calendar, *panchanga*.

Aryabhata's works were later adopted by the Greeks and Arabs, and translated into Latin during the thirteenth century. It was from these works that the Europeans learned how to calculate the area and volume of triangles and squares.

To recognize the contribution of this extraordinary scientist, the first Indian satellite of India was named after him. Astronomers have also named a lunar crater after this genius. ARIES—the Aryabhata Research Institute of Observational Sciences, near Nainital, has been established to carry out research in atmospheric sciences, astrophysics and astronomy. The Aryabhata Inter-School Mathematics Competition is a prestigious event conducted annually for students of classes' five to eight. A species of bacteria, the Bacillus Aryabhata discovered in 2009, has been named after this extraordinary innovator.

Due to his innovative theories and perfect calculations, Aryabhata is admired by mathematicians even now, centuries after his life and times.

The Great Emperor

Name: Ashoka
Birth Date: 304 BC
Place: Pataliputra
Death Date: 232 BC
Place: Pataliputra, Bihar

A little boy, six years old, tiptoed behind his grandfather in the royal garden, almost sprinting to keep up with him on the dusty path as the first rays of the sun shone through the trees. The old man was clad in white cloth from shoulder to knee and walked with long, measured steps, like a monk. His right hand clutched something to his chest. As his grandfather reached a clearing, stopped and turned around, the boy ducked behind a bush just in time to avoid being noticed. Grandpa raised his right hand, revealing a glimpse of the leather scabbard in his hand. He paused for a moment and then spoke in a calm voice: 'You have helped me conquer the world and become an emperor. But I, Chandragupta Maurya, have realized that one's real victory is conquering oneself, one's desires and passions. And no sword can help me there. Now on,

I am a Jain monk and will spend the rest of my life trying to achieve that final victory before I renounce the world. Off you go!'

He hurled his sword. It spun through the air and crashed against a nearby tree. As the old emperor turned back, something in blue robes and a red turban dashed past him towards the sword. Before he could say, 'Ashoka, what are you doing here?', the little boy had picked up the sword. 'It's mine! I will conquer the world with it,' said little Ashoka, with childlike exuberance.

'I won't stop you if you want to keep it,' said Chandragupta, 'but let me warn you that, at the end of the day, you won't be happy with it.'

Chandragupta was right.

While historians might differ on specific aspects of Ashoka's life, they are unanimous in pronouncing him as one of the greatest and noblest rulers that India has ever known.

Though born into one of the richest royal lineages of ancient India, the Mauryan empire, early life was not easy for Ashoka. His grandfather Chandragupta Maurya and father Bindusara had built up a huge empire including a major part of what is today the Indian subcontinent. However, like in any other royal house, the Mauryan brothers were at loggerheads after Bindusara's death. Only the fiercest and most valiant of them, Ashoka, survived by crushing all his rivals.

There was no stopping Ashoka once he ascended the

throne and made Magadha his capital. He launched campaign after campaign to usurp free kingdoms outside his reign, ruthlessly wiping out all those who stood in his way, thus earning the nickname Chandashok ('terrible Ashoka').

For eight years, the juggernaut rolled, stretching the boundaries of the Mauryan empire from the border of Iran in the west to Assam in the east; from the Pamir Knots in the north to Andhra Pradesh and parts of Tamil Nadu in the south. It was only at Kalinga (now Orissa) that the victory march of his sword met an unlikely end—not by defeat, but by transformation.

Following Kalinga's refusal to surrender, Ashoka's army destroyed the kingdom, killing 1,00,000 people and taking another 1,50,000 people captive. Legend says that when he roamed the city a day after the plunder, Ashoka was greeted by vultures and crows feasting on corpses strewn across a burnt kingdom. Anyone left alive had lost a dear one; his army hadn't spared even women and infants. Remorse filled his heart at the sight, making him wonder if this were really victory. That was the end of his brutality. Chandashoka had made way for Dhammashoka, who would win not by the sword but by righteousness.

Shortly after Kalinga, Ashoka embraced Buddhism, adopting the precepts of Dharma, which included ahimsa (non-violence), tolerance of all sects, respect for teachers and priests, obedience to parents, and humane treatment of everyone. The reformed Ashoka set out on a holistic development plan for his kingdom. He built universities, renovated major roads throughout India, and developed irrigation and water transit systems to help commerce and agriculture. He also built hospitals for animal care. Perhaps his biggest contribution was elevating the status of Buddhism to a true world religion, by sending messengers throughout and beyond the Indian subcontinent. Mahindra and Sanghamitra, his son and daughter, are known to have travelled to Sri Lanka and converted the island nation's king to Buddhism.

Ashoka's voice can still be heard in the numerous rock and pillar inscriptions and edicts he had commissioned. The etchings represent India's first intelligible written script, since the Indus Valley script is as yet undeciphered. It is only befitting that the Lion Capital from the pillar at Sarnath has been adopted as the national emblem of India.

Nationalist and Yogi

Name: Aurobindo Ghosh
Birth Date: 15 August 1872
Place: Calcutta (now Kolkata), West Bengal
Death Date: 5 December 1950
Place: Pondicherry

In 1907, when the Indian freedom movement was gathering momentum, Nobel laureate Rabindranath Tagore visited Aurobindo and said: 'Rabindranath, O Aurobindo, bows to thee! O friend, my country's friend, O voice incarnate, free, of India's soul. . . The fiery messenger that with the lamp of God hath come. . . Rabindranath, O Aurobindo, bows to thee.'

In 1928, when Aurobindo left politics to pursue spirituality, Tagore said: 'You have the Word and we are waiting to accept it from you. India will speak through your voice to the world!'

A fiery revolutionary and patriot, a brilliant scholar and philosopher, and a spiritual guru and yogi in his later years—Aurobindo was a multifaceted personality. He was best described by his close spiritual collaborator Mirra Alfassa, known universally as the Mother. She said: 'What Sri Aurobindo represents in the world's history is not a teaching, not even a revelation; it is a decisive action direct from the Supreme.'

This yogi was born as Aurobindo Ackroyd Ghosh to Swarnalata Devi and Dr Krishna Dhan Ghosh. His mother was the daughter of a famous Brahmo Samaj social reformer and his father was the district surgeon of Rangapur in Bengal. Dr Ghosh was also an Anglophile who was fascinated by Western thought and culture. This is evident from the middle name that he gave his son Aurobindo in honour of his friend Annette Ackroyd.

Young Aurobindo began his education at Loreto Convent School, Darjeeling. Two years later, his father sent him to England for a 'complete' Western education. Aurobindo was first tutored by his father's friends, Mrs and Rev. Drewett, with whom he lived in Manchester. There he developed a love for poetry that lasted throughout his life.

In 1884, Aurobindo shifted to London and continued his education at St Paul's. He developed an interest in Western literature and mastered many languages including French, Italian, Spanish, Greek and Latin. Those were the toughest years of his life because the allowances he received from his father were either insufficient or very irregular. There were days when he had to go without dinner or a warm coat to protect himself from the severe London winter. But Aurobindo was unfazed. He pursued his studies diligently. He was rewarded with the Butterworth Prize for Literature, the Bedford Prize for History as well as a scholarship to Cambridge. In 1890, aged eighteen, he entered Cambridge, where again he proved to be brilliant in academics.

While at Cambridge, Aurobindo received news of the nationalist movement gaining ground in India. Although his formative years were spent in England, he had not developed any attachment to that country. He returned to India and served as a civil servant in Baroda. Then he became a professor of French and finally the vice-principal of Baroda College.

Meanwhile, he also joined the freedom struggle. He believed in direct political action against the British. Moderate reformism was not for him. He became the editor of the revolutionary Bengali newspaper, *Bande Mataram*, and contributed provocative articles that landed him in jail. He wrote for other magazines as well. In an article published in a Bombay weekly, *Induprakash*, he wrote: 'Our actual enemy is not any force exterior to ourselves, but our own crying weaknesses, our cowardice, our selfishness, our hypocrisy, our purblind sentimentalism.'

Aurobindo's spiritual nature developed in parallel with his nationalism, as he contributed writings on yoga and meditation as well. Incidentally, it was in jail that he had a divine spiritual experience in the form of a vision of the all-pervading reality. This changed his life. After he was released, he quit politics in 1910 and went to Pondicherry to pursue yoga and spirituality, and to write books and poetry. *The Life Divine*, *Essays on Gita*, *The Synthesis of Yoga*, and *Savitri* are some of his famous works.

Sri Aurobindo had several intense spiritual experiences. Once when asked by his guru, Vishnu Bhaskara Lele, to try for silence as part of yogic preparations, he achieved silence in the mind in a mere three days. Most yogis require months to achieve this. At another time, he had a vision of Swami Vivekananda, who appeared before him in jail and asked him to read the Bhagavad Gita. Swamiji also showed him the existence of the Supermind and told him to seek that as his goal.

In Pondicherry, Aurobindo met Mirra Alfassa, wife of French diplomat Paul Richard, who became his ardent spiritual follower. Later, Mirra was to become the Mother, who played a central role in creating the Aurobindo Ashram and Auroville in Pondicherry.

Sri Aurobindo taught us the possibility of transforming world consciousness through the spiritual journey of discipline and yoga. According to him, a receptive mind can, through discipline, can attain realization. The chief aim of education should be to help the growing soul to draw out that in itself which is best and make it perfect for noble use.

Perhaps, the most fitting description of Aurobindo was given by A.B. Clark, principal of Baroda College: 'So you met Aurobindo Ghosh. Did you notice his eyes? There is a mystic fire and light in them. They penetrate into the beyond.' Clark added, 'If Joan of Arc heard heavenly voices, Aurobindo probably sees heavenly visions.'

Sri Aurobindo passed away on 5 December 1950. The Mother continued spreading his message of consciousness evolution and organized the spiritual community known as Sri Aurobindo Ashram. The city of Auroville was also established in accordance with his ideals.

The Humble Business Tycoon

Name: Azim Premji
Birth Date: 24 July 1945
Place: Bombay Presidency, British India

Reserved and reclusive, he prefers to keep a low profile and avoids media attention as much as possible. He is also known to travel economy class and stay in his own company guest houses rather than in luxury hotels. However, on more than one occasion, he has made it to the *Forbes* list of richest Indians. That's Azim Premji, as famous for his frugal lifestyle as he is for his astonishing wealth.

When Premji was once asked how it felt to be India's richest person, he replied that he felt like an animal in a zoo. He said that he resented the fact that people focused so much on his wealth, as though there were nothing more to him beyond that. This incident pretty much sums up his discomfort with ostentation and hype.

Azim Premji comes from a Gujarati business family. His father owned a company called Western India

Products, which later became known as Wipro. The company manufactured consumer care products, such as hydrogenated vegetable oils and fats.

Premji completed his initial education in Mumbai. When he was pursuing his electrical engineering course at Stanford University, his father suddenly passed away. At the age of twenty, Premji had to give up his studies and return to India to take over the family business. However, he proved equal to the challenge.

Under Premji's leadership, the company diversified into many new segments including toiletries, lighting products, hydraulic cylinders and information technology (IT). Among all these, the IT business grew rapidly. Soon, a large proportion of the company's revenues were being generated by this division. Wipro was catapulted into the global league of the fastest expanding companies and, along with it, Premji's wealth also grew.

Such rapid and mercurial success, however, did not affect Premji's simple ways or humble demeanour. Instead, it prompted him to use whatever means he could for the benefit of society. Premji strongly believes that private organizations have a social responsibility. One of his prime concerns is the improvement of education facilities in India, particularly primary education. In 2001, he set up the Azim Premji Foundation, a non-profit organization that seeks to provide quality primary education to every child. He has been involved in numerous other philanthropic initiatives since then.

Premji has delivered several inspirational speeches in academic institutions across India. 'The Changing World', his speech on the subject of change at the Indian Institute of Management, Ahmedabad, has been popularized through the Internet and inspires many people.

In some of his speeches, Premji has dwelt on values such as humility, perseverance, excellence, focusing on one's strengths and dealing with adversity. On other occasions, he has spoken of how his success has largely been due to the respect he has for his competitors and his willingness to learn from them rather than underestimate them.

Never one to give up easily, Premji completed his degree in electrical engineering in 1999. Remember, circumstances had forced him to drop out of it thirty years earlier.

In 2003, *Forbes* listed him as one of the ten most effective people around the globe, who have the 'power to effect change'. In 2007, *Business Week* listed him in the top thirty entrepreneurs in world history. Premji has been awarded an honorary doctorate from Wesleyan University in Connecticut for his philanthropic work. He is also a recipient of the Padma Bhushan.

The Fiery Freedom Fighter

Name: Bal Gangadhar Tilak
Birth Date: 23 July 1856
Place: Ratnagiri, Maharashtra
Death Date: 1 August 1920
Place: Bombay, British India

'Swaraj is my birthright and I shall have it!' Bal Gangadhar Tilak is probably best known among the masses in India for this slogan. Tilak was one of the strongest proponents of swaraj or 'self-government' for India. He felt this was the only way to free Indians, who were at the receiving end of the unjust policies of British colonizers.

Tilak had founded a Marathi newspaper called *Kesari* ('The Lion'), through which he lashed out against several injustices meted out by the British. As a result, the British government arrested him on several occasions for speaking out against them. One such occasion was in 1908.

Tilak had just written an article defending some Indian youths who had attacked certain British individuals. Tilak was arrested and sentenced for six years to a Burmese prison. On hearing the ruling, Tilak is believed to have said, 'In spite of the jury's verdict, I maintain that I am innocent. There are higher powers that rule the destiny of men and nations and it may be the will of providence that the cause I represent may prosper more by my suffering than by my remaining free.'

This fiery individual was labelled the 'Father of the Indian Unrest' by the British, who had a tough time trying to curb his role in the Indian Independence movement.

Tilak started off as a mathematics teacher in Pune before turning to journalism. He founded the Deccan Education Society along with some of his friends to inculcate awareness of Indian culture and values in the youth. He believed that the education system then did not focus on these aspects adequately. Soon, Tilak became actively involved in the freedom movement and joined the Indian National Congress. Being a man of extreme views, he had quite a few differences with other freedom fighters, who felt that some amount of moderation should be exercised even when fighting for the country.

However, there were others who admired Tilak's strong views and temperament, which he expressed through his writing. In fact, *Kesari* achieved great popularity in a short span of time. 'Be sure of your facts. Let your words be clear as daylight.' Those were

Tilak's words to his fellow journalists. He also founded an English newspaper called *The Maratha*.

Not limiting himself to revolutionary journalism, Tilak also authored a number of books on other subjects, such as *Oorayan*, written during his time in prison. *The Arctic Home in the Vedas* is one of his influential works on the origin of the Aryans.

On his release from prison in Burma, Tilak joined some other freedom fighters to form the All India Home Rule League, which sought self-government for India within the British empire.

Though Tilak was a strong critic of Gandhi's non-violent methods, Gandhiji respected his work and is believed to have referred to Tilak as 'The Maker of Modern India'.

Apart from his role in the freedom movement, Tilak is known for popularizing Ganesh Chaturthi in Maharashtra. With his encouragement, the festival that was usually celebrated in homes turned into a large-scale public event where people celebrated together. Through such actions, apart from his writing, Tilak stirred Indian minds and inculcated in people a sense of pride for their traditions and their own, indigenous, national way of life.

Appropriately, Tilak is often referred to as 'Lokmanya', which means revered by the people.

Performer and Guru Par Excellence

Name: Birju Maharaj
Birth Date: 4 February 1938
Place: Lucknow, Uttar Pradesh

At the tender age of three, he would spend hours watching his father Acchan Maharaj, an accomplished Kathak dancer, teach his students. Music and dance fascinated this little child. Gifted as he was, he had even learnt a few complex musical pieces that accompanied the dance movements in the classroom—all through mere observation.

Noticing his young son's talent and love for arts, Acchan Maharaj formally initiated him into training in dance. Thus was nurtured one of the most spectacular and well-known Kathak performers the world has ever seen—Birju Maharaj.

Birju Maharaj's first public performance was at the age of seven. His father passed away not long after, when the boy was just nine. However, coming from a family of Kathak dancers—the Kalka Bindadin Gharana of Lucknow—he was fortunate enough to be taken into the tutelage of his uncles, who ensured that his rapid rise was not stalled by the demise of his father.

Over the years, Birju Maharaj's reputation grew by leaps and bounds. He became known not only as a mesmerizing performer but also as a teacher par excellence. Starting with his first teaching job at Sangeet Bharti in Delhi at the age of thirteen, he went on to teach at several other organizations before setting up his own dance school, Kalashram, in Delhi. Apart from teaching at Kalashram, he also conducts lecture demonstrations and workshops across the world.

Birju Maharaj's talent and efforts have been lauded not just by the Indian government but also by other institutions and nations. He received the Sangeet Natak Academi Award when he was just twenty-eight. He has also been honoured with the Padma Vibhushan, the Kalidas Samman and the Soviet Land Nehru Award. These are just some of the countless citations and awards he has received in his illustrious career. The maestro has been conferred with an honorary doctorate from Benares Hindu University.

Laurels galore cannot outshine the allure he holds for thousands of his devoted fans, both Indian and international, who come to watch his performances and demonstrations, or travel across continents to learn from him.

Apart from his renditions of pure Kathak pieces, Birju Maharaj is known for applying Kathak forms and techniques to dance dramas, thus taking the classical dance form to the masses. In his dance dramas, such as *Geet Govind, Malhar* and *Dasavataar* he addresses traditional as well as contemporary themes. He has also choreographed dance sequences for Hindi movies, such as Satyajit Ray's *Shatranj Ke Khiladi* and Sanjay Leela Bhansali's *Devdas*.

Not many people know that Birju Maharaj is also an excellent singer, adept at rendering thumris, bhajans, ghazals, and other forms of vocal music. He also plays several stringed instruments and drums, most of these skills being self-taught. Another little known fact is that Birju Maharaj also composed music and sang for the dance sequence that he choreographed in *Shatranj Ke Khiladi*. He also composed music for *Devdas*.

The depth and range of Birju Maharaj's multifaceted personality does not end here. An excellent orator, he intersperses his lectures and workshops with anecdotes from his extraordinary life as well as observations on contemporary issues, enthralling his audiences.

Birju Maharaj is wholly dedicated to his craft to this day, and continues to play a phenomenal role in keeping the vibrant dance form of Kathak alive.

The Man Who Fought Against the Tide

Name: B.R. Ambedkar
Birth Date: 14 April 1891
Place: Mhow, Central Provinces (now in Madhya Pradesh)
Death Date: 6 December 1956
Place: Delhi

In the first issue of the weekly Marathi newspaper *Mooknayak* ('Leader of the Voiceless') which Dr Bhimrao Ramji Ambedkar founded in 1920, he called India a 'home of inequality'. He also described Hindu society as 'a tower which had several storeys without a ladder or an entrance. One was to die in the storey in which one was born'.

This was his way of expressing his angst against the hierarchical caste system of the Hindus, in which the so-called 'upper' castes discriminated against those they perceived as 'lower' castes. In those days, there was no way a lower-caste person could aspire to have the same facilities and opportunities as an upper-caste person. In *Mooknayak*, Ambedkar used the analogy of a multistoreyed tower to describe this state of affairs.

Ambedkar himself was born into one of the lowest rungs of the caste hierarchy and was therefore considered an 'untouchable'. As a result, at school, Ambedkar had to suffer many humiliating situations. Many of his classmates, who belonged to upper castes, refused to sit anywhere near him. Students like him were not even allowed to drink water from the same sources as them. In fact, several teachers, too, refused to come close to him and other untouchable students.

Even in these challenging and heartbreaking circumstances, Ambedkar excelled as a student and even passed his tenth standard examination. Since the lower castes hardly got equal opportunities for a decent education and were often neglected by the teachers, the chances of them reaching this level were extremely rare—so rare that when Ambedkar actually accomplished this feat, the members of his community wanted to organize a celebration in his honour.

Due to his exceptional academic qualities, Ambedkar received scholarships to pursue his degree at Bombay University and then further studies at Columbia University in the US. During his stint in the US, for the first time, Ambedkar felt liberated from the oppressive caste-ridden environment he had faced all his life. Having experienced such freedom, he felt all the more stifled when he returned to India after a few years and saw that things had not changed much. He was still considered an 'untouchable' in his own country.

To support himself, Ambedkar worked briefly as a private tutor and went on to become a professor at Sydenham College in Bombay. Here too, he faced discrimination from his own professional colleagues, though he was largely accepted by his students. He later went to London to pursue further studies in economics and law. On his return to India this time, he set up a legal practice, which soon flourished.

Eventually, Ambedkar became actively involved in India's political life. He took part in public movements and marches and utilized every platform and opportunity to fight vehemently for the rights of the oppressed lower castes. He received more opposition than support for his endeavour, yet he did not give up. Being a person of immense intellect and scholarly accomplishments, he also wrote several books on the caste system to make people aware of its inhuman nature. Some of his well-known works are *The Annihilation of Caste* and *Who were the Shudras?*

Towards the end of his life, he converted to Buddhism, which he felt was a religion that encouraged equality among people. Also known as Babasaheb, Ambedkar was instrumental in the drafting of the Indian Constitution, a much-admired document which, among other things, advocates equal rights for all citizens of the country. He was awarded the Bharat Ratna posthumously, in 1990.

The Fearless Revolutionary

Name: Chandrashekhar Sitaram Tiwari
Birth Date: 23 July 1906
Place: Badarka, Uttar Pradesh
Death Date: 27 February 1931
Place: Alfred Park, Allahabad, Uttar Pradesh

The Jallianwala Bagh Massacre of 1919 shook up this dynamic teenager and became a turning point in his life. He pledged to participate actively in the freedom struggle and engaged himself in various revolutionary activities. He also supported the Non-Cooperation Movement launched by Mahatma Gandhi.

He received the first punishment for his ardent patriotism at the age of fifteen. When he was brought to court, the magistrate asked him his name. 'Azad!' (Freedom), he replied proudly. When he was questioned further, he said that his father was *Swatantra* (independence), his mother was *Dharti Ma* (earth) and his residence was the prison. The provoked magistrate sentenced him to fifteen lashes. At every stroke of the whip, he shouted, 'Bharat mata ki jai!'

Chandrashekhar   Sitaram   Tiwari   became
Chandrashekhar Azad after this remarkable incident.
Azad was the son of Jagrani Devi and Pandit Sita Ram
Tiwari. He spent his initial years in Bhavra district
where he received his schooling and then went to
Varanasi for higher studies.

Azad vowed that he would die as a free individual and
would never allow the British to arrest him during his
lifetime. When the Non-Cooperation Movement was
suspended by Gandhiji, Azad went on his own path,
as he believed in aggressive revolution and was willing
to use arms and weapons to fight for independence.
The masses worshipped his valour. Understandably,
the British government detested him and was always
on the lookout for this fierce warrior.

To escape from the police, Azad disguised himself as
a priest and spent a few years in Jhansi. Hence, he was
fondly called Panditji. A staunch believer in socialistic
principles, Azad mentored many young revolutionaries
like Bhagat Singh, Rajguru and Sukhdev and went on to
form the Hindustan Socialist Republican Association

A notable incident involving Azad was the notorious
Kakori train robbery where he looted the coins of the
British treasury. Other acts in which he was involved
were the Assembly bombing, the Delhi conspiracy, the
Lahore shooting to avenge the death of Lala Lajpat
Rai (where J.P. Saunders fell to his bullets) and the
attempt to bomb the Viceroy's train. These incidents
intimidated the British, who announced a hefty cash

prize for anyone who would capture Azad, dead or alive.

In 1931, a police informer betrayed Azad and invited him to the Alfred Park in Allahabad after notifying the British officials. The police force surrounded the park and ordered Azad to surrender. Rising to the occasion, Azad fought single-handedly till he had just one bullet left in his pistol. He then shot himself, keeping his word that he would never be arrested by the British during his lifetime.

Alfred Park is now known as Chandrashekhar Azad Park. Films have been made on the courageous struggle put up by Azad in league with Bhagat Singh, Ashfaqulla Khan and Ram Prasad Bismil. Azad's heroism inspires millions of Indians who salute this brave martyr for sacrificing his life for his country at such a young age.

The Knighted Scientist

Name: Chandrasekara Venkata Raman
Birth Date: 7 November 1888
Place: Tiruchirappalli, Tamil Nadu
Death Date: 21 November 1970
Place: Bangalore, Karnataka

The world of physics fascinated this young scientist so much that he challenged geographical isolation and fought off political oppression to prove the potential of Indians in research through his valuable contribution.

Despite his limited opportunities and facilities, he ushered India into the world of modern science. Fortunately, his work did not go unrecognized globally and he became the first Indian, the first Asian and the first non-white to win the coveted Nobel Prize in Physics for discovering the Raman Effect in 1930.

C.V. Raman was the youngest undergraduate admitted into Presidency College with a scholarship. His teachers found him to be brilliant and knowledgeable. He conducted experiments on diffraction of light and, at the age of eighteen, published a paper in a prestigious scientific research journal in London. He graduated with a gold medal in physics. Later he completed his post graduation with flying colours from the same institution.

During this time, Raman did not find any suitable research opportunities to pursue his interest in physics. Meanwhile, he topped the civil services examination and was appointed assistant accounts general at Calcutta. Before taking up his first job, he married Lokasundari Ammal who was then just thirteen years old.

One day, on his way to work, Raman noticed a board that read 'Indian Association for Cultivation of Sciences'. He sought permission from the concerned officials to use the facilities of the institute to conduct his experiments. Excited at the prospect of pursuing research, Raman put in several hours of work, which ultimately paved the way for transforming the scientific culture of our nation.

Raman's vision for the development of science gradually expanded and he started a bulletin to publish original works by scientists. This later became the *Indian Journal of Physics*, one of the most prestigious scientific journals in the world, which is still being published.

Raman's inquisitive nature perceived every natural phenomenon that would go unnoticed by an average individual. Right from the whispering gallery at St Paul's Cathedral to the sound of musical instruments such as the *tabla* to the marvellous blue colour of the sea, for each and every observation he made, Raman came up with interesting scientific explanations.

In 1917, when he was offered the Tarakanath Palit Professorship for physics at Calcutta University,

Raman gave up government service to accept the post. At the same time, he carried on study and research at the Indian Association for the Cultivation of Science.

Raman was confident of his research calibre and the originality of his work. When he discovered the Raman Effect, he was so sure of winning the Nobel Prize that he had actually booked tickets for himself and his wife to Sweden much before the announcement was made!

To honour the discovery of the Raman Effect in 1928 and to commemorate the invaluable contribution of this legend who brought international recognition to modern Indian science, our country celebrates 28 February as National Science Day.

Raman was truly a patriot. He discouraged Indian intellectuals from travelling abroad to pursue higher studies or research. Instead, when he became the director of the Indian Institute of Science, he invited physicists from overseas to conduct their experiments here.

In 1934, he founded and became the first president of the Indian Academy of Sciences and served his tenure until his last days. To recognize his commitment and dedication to promoting scientific research in India, this organization has now set up the Raman Chair, which is occupied on invitation by eminent scientists.

Raman was a member of many prestigious scientific societies and a recipient of numerous honorary doctorates. He was awarded a knighthood in 1929 and the prestigious Bharat Ratna in 1954. Raman has earned a permanent position of eminence in the world of science.

Reformer of Religion

Name: Dayanand Saraswati
Birth Date: 12 February 1824
Place: Morvi, Gujarat
Death Date: 31 October 1883
Place: Ajmer, Rajasthan

Mulshankar, as Swami Dayanand Saraswati was called in his boyhood, once attended a community Shivratri prayer with his parents. As per the custom, devotees were to stay awake through the night and immerse themselves in worship. However, as the night progressed, they gradually began to doze off. Young Mulshankar remained alert. Soon, he noticed some mice near the *shivalinga*. They were eating the food kept there as an offering to the lord. Mulshankar was struck by how powerless the idol was in stopping the mice, even though he had often heard that god is an all-powerful force. This incident had a deep impact on his mind, and such experiences led him to question the merits of idol worship later in his life.

Mulshankar's probing mind did not allow him to accept anything blindly. In due course, he became one of India's foremost social reformers, questioning and opposing many practices of the time, including the purdah system, child marriage, ritualistic forms of worship and untouchability. He strongly supported equal rights for men and women.

The roots of his later beliefs can be traced to his childhood. Even as a young boy, Mulshankar gave much thought to matters like life and death. As he grew older, he became more and more detached from materialistic life. This detachment heightened when he witnessed the deaths of his sister and a beloved uncle. At the age of twenty-two, he left home and wandered about the country in search of a teacher who could guide him towards the right path.

Many years later, he finally found the person who he came to accept as his guru—Swami Virajananda. Guided by him, Dayanand Saraswati embarked on an in-depth study of the Vedas, the ancient Indian texts. There are several stories of his unwavering devotion and loyalty towards his guru.

Dayanand Saraswati came to believe strongly in the Hindu religion as depicted in the Vedas. He felt that the form of Hinduism practised by the people in his time was not true to the Vedas; in fact, it had been corrupted by the self-serving interests of the priestly class. Moreover, several superstitious beliefs and unjust practices had entered the Hinduism ideology.

After the period of his study with his guru, Dayanand Saraswati set about reforming Hinduism. He wanted to eliminate the ills that had crept into the religion and restore the faith to its pure form, as depicted in the Vedas. He founded an institution called the Arya Samaj to spread his thoughts and reform society. He also wrote commentaries and tracts on ethics and morality. Some of his major works are *Satyarth Prakash* and *Sanskarvidhi*.

During his travels across India, he participated in debates with people of diverse religious views, trying to help them understand his interpretation of religion and social issues. Some who heard him were deeply inspired by his thoughts and teachings. Others were angered by his ways and even plotted to kill him. Dayanand Saraswati, however, stuck to his beliefs and fearlessly spoke his mind even in the face of vehement opposition. Eventually, he was poisoned by a cook during his stay with the Maharaja of Jodhpur and passed away some days later.

The remarkable thing, however, is that Swami Dayanand Saraswati not only forgave the person who had poisoned him but also provided the culprit with enough money to make a quick escape before he could be punished by his employer for his act of treachery.

Upanyas Samrat

Name: Dhanpat Rai
Birth Date: 31 July 1880
Place: Lamahi, Uttar Pradesh
Death Date: 8 October 1936
Place: Varanasi, Uttar Pradesh

Dhanpat Rai, who is more widely known by his pen name, Munshi Premchand, was once asked why he didn't write anything about himself, though he wrote about so many other people and issues. 'What greatness do I have that I have to tell anyone about?' Premchand replied. 'I live just like millions of people in this country. I am ordinary. My life is also ordinary. I am a poor schoolteacher suffering family travails. In my whole life, I have been grinding away with the hope that I could be free of my sufferings. But I have not been able to free myself from suffering. What is so special about this life that needs to be told to anybody?'

The fact that Premchand could identify so closely with common people and their struggles was perhaps the reason why he was able to depict their lives in such a realistic manner in his writings. One of the greatest

Hindi–Urdu writers of the 20th century, Premchand addressed a range of contemporary social issues in his short stories and novels. Poverty often provides the stark undercurrent to several of his stories.

Just like the memorable characters he etched out, Premchand led a life of strife and struggle. His parents died when he was young. He had a stepmother and siblings to support. Moreover, he had an ill-fated arranged marriage at the age of fourteen, which ended a few years later.

Premchand left his village when he was nineteen to take up a teaching job in another village. He supported his family with his meagre income. Later, he taught at a government school in Varanasi, before being appointed headmaster of an Allahabad school. Two years later, he became the deputy sub-inspector of schools in Kanpur.

It was during his Allahabad stint that Premchand began writing. He published short stories, novels and columns in Urdu newspapers and magazines under the pen name Nawab Rai. He got into trouble with the publication of *Soz-e-Watan* ('Dirge of the Nation'), his anthology of Urdu short stories. British officials confiscated and destroyed all copies of the book, as they felt its contents would kindle nationalism among the common people. In the wake of this, he changed his pen name to Premchand and started writing increasingly in Hindi. The form of Hindi he used was closer to the form used by common people in their everyday lives, not the erudite, literary and sophisticated version used by scholars and writers of the time. He wrote some works for children like *Manmodak* and *Jangal Ki Kahaniyan*. He also edited literary–political magazines like *Jagran* and *Hans*.

Premchand's reputation as a writer grew steadily and he carved a distinct niche for himself in literary circles. *Nirmala*, *Godaan* and *Sevasadan* are his notable works. However, writing did not earn him wealth. He continued to struggle to make ends meet. Remarkably, his struggles seem to have fuelled his creativity rather than curbing it. Also remarkable is the fact that Premchand didn't just talk about social ills—he also set an example in social reform through the steps he took in his life. In 1909, for instance, when widow remarriage was considered taboo, he married a widow called Shivrani.

Premchand's writings have touched the hearts of many. Renowned film-maker Satyajit Ray created two masterpieces, *Sadgati* and *Shatranj Ke Khiladi*, based on Premchand's works. His stories continue to charm millions of readers today and are often dramatised.

Champion of Indian Hockey

Name: Dhanraj Pillay
Birth Date: 16 July 1968
Place: Pune, Maharashtra

This champion player placed India's national game on the global charts by leading his squad to victory in several international tournaments. His ardent fervour for hockey and his tireless zeal even when he was on the verge of complete exhaustion helped him grab victory time and again. Off field, he stood for his principles and for the game he loves. During his twelve-year stint, he paid a heavy price for questioning the authorities and bureaucrats, and bringing stunning facts out into the open.

Dhanraj Pillay ruled the field for over a decade with his charisma. The national game of hockey has become personified with this dynamic captain. During his career, Dhanraj oscillated continuously between victories and defeats. Moments of pain and pride went hand in hand.

Dhanraj played in four Olympics, four World Cups and four Asian Games. He also showed his emotions openly on the field, whether his team lost or won. At the Sydney Olympics 2000, when India lost narrowly in the semi-finals, he cried inconsolably on the field. On the other hand, when his team won against Pakistan in a challenging game at the Champions Trophy, he knelt down and mouthed silent thanks.

During one such victorious return to the homeland, no senior official from the Indian Hockey Federation (IHF) was present to receive the team at the airport late at night. The hockey champions spent the entire night at the airport with their medals. Along with the coach and goalkeeper, Dhanraj spoke out openly against this shabby treatment. Needless to say, he was dropped from the next tournament.

The repercussions of being frank and forthright before the media almost sealed his career. Dhanraj was considered rebellious when he boldly exposed bare truths. However, he did not regret fighting against the IHF for the development of the game and the players. He still gets emotional when he talks about his lone struggle and is thankful for his family's support during this ordeal.

Dhanraj Pillay also brought to light the low stipend paid to the players. He was backed by his entire team and they refused to go on an international tour until their demands were met. The officials convinced them and promised to increase the settlement on return.

Unfortunatly, even now, Indian hockey players get much lower remuneration compared to those in other countries.

Struggles were not new to this gifted sportsman. Hailing from a very humble family background, he was used to practising with broken hockey sticks in the neighbourhood of an armament factory where his family had settled. Later, he went through formal training in Pune before being selected to play at the international level. Dhanraj never forgets to acknowledge the sacrifices his mother made to help him turn his dream into reality.

Dhanraj started a hockey academy in Mumbai to support and train talented players, irrespective of financial or racial background. As a new initiative, the team collected used printer cartridges and sold them to raise funds for the academy. However, the academy had to later close down due to insufficient funds.

Today, Dhanraj has gathered fans not only in his home town Pune but also all over India and abroad. Every hockey-loving nation including Germany and Pakistan looks forward to watching him on the field. Even at the age of forty, aided by his magical stick and his uncanny ability to take opponents by surprise, he can give younger and more energetic players a run for their money.

Pillay has received the Padma Shri and the Rajiv Gandhi Khel Ratna. He has served as the manager of the national hockey team. His latest venture has been playing for Karnataka in the World Series Hockey.

Despite a controversial career, Pillay still stands as a pillar of hope—the hope of a whole new dimension to India's national game. Though hockey players still do not enjoy the limelight they deserve, his passion and sheer love for hockey is undaunted. He hopes that upcoming players will take the game to a new level by showing their spark on the field, consistently.

The Polyester Prince

Name: Dhirajlal Hirachand Ambani
Birth Date: 28 December 1932
Place: Chorwad, British India (now Gujarat)
Death Date: 6 July 2002
Place: Mumbai, Maharashtra

This brilliant businessman dared to dream about expanding boundaries and thereby rewrote India's corporate history by challenging the bureaucracy. He revolutionized the rules of running a business and manipulated the existing system to his advantage, leaving no stone unturned while grabbing opportunities that came his way.

What he finally achieved in his lifetime still remains only a dream for tycoons all over the world. He almost single-handedly built a global business empire, disregarding all criticisms and accusations about his unethical modus operandi. While he did enjoy a great degree of clout in political circles, at some points in his adventurous journey, controversies surrounded him so much that they took a toll on his health and his achievements seemed dwarfed.

However, Ambani also won the hearts of his workers. He was approachable and helpful, and allowed his employees to speak to him directly about any issue. He adopted a unique approach while handling shareholders, journalists, as well as other government officials, and challenged anybody who questioned his growth.

Dhirubhai Ambani was born to a village school-teacher in Gujarat. His alert and intelligent mind was extremely active even in his young days when he constantly thought of effective ways to earn more money to cater to the needs of his family. He found it nearly impossible to sit in a classroom following lessons. Instead, he believed in action and started his modest business by setting up stalls at village fairs to earn that extra income.

During his teens, he shifted to Aden and worked as a clerk for a meagre salary. At that time, silver was in high demand in London. Since the Yemen rial was made of silver, Dhirubhai melted the currency and sold it as metal to London traders.

After making a marginal profit, he returned to India, rented a modest single bedroom flat and started a venture along with his cousin. They imported polyester yarn and exported spices. The duo started Reliance Commercial Corporation in a one-room office with just three chairs, a table and a telephone. Due to differences in their basic temperaments and business ethics, the cousins, however, soon parted ways.

Dhirubhai did not fear taking risks. He foresaw the future and prepared himself to make huge profits. In a few years, he shifted to a posh apartment and established himself as a successful businessman. Dhirubhai's business acumen was odd but unique. He exported at a loss and made huge profits from his imports. He always imported goods that were high in demand.

Dhirubhai started his first textile mill that produced high-quality polyester fibre, which he sold under the brand Vimal. Using his aggressive marketing skills and by encouraging retail franchise outlets to sell only this brand, he turned Vimal into a household name.

During the late 1970s, he successfully convinced more than 50,000 investors to become shareholders of Reliance. He included even the small investors from the rural areas of Gujarat to subscribe to the initial public offering. Within a few years, Reliance Industries expanded so much that the annual meetings had to be conducted in stadiums.

By the early 1980s, Dhirubhai was already a millionaire. Around the same time, the company diversified into various spheres like plastics, petrochemicals, and power. Reliance Industries had become a huge empire with a yearly turnover of over ten billion rupees and employed almost 85,000 people. During the 1990s, the company forayed into telecommunications also.

Extreme business pressure and constant opposition

from political and judicial circles took a toll on this businessman, and in the year 2002 he suffered a massive stroke that paralysed his right hand. However, Dhirubhai's mind was as agile as ever. His two sons, Mukesh and Anil, managed the business affairs during this crisis. His second major stroke in 2002 pushed him into coma for a week and eventually claimed his life.

After his death, his sons had differences over ownership issues, which were resolved by Dhirubhai's wife Kokilaben. The empire was then split into two. Mukesh became the head of Reliance Industries Limited taking over IPCL and RIL, while Anil took on the responsibility of spearheading Reliance ADA Group, comprising Reliance Infocomm, Reliance Energy and Reliance Capital.

The Father of Indian Cinema

Name: Dhundiraj Govind Phalke
Birth Date: 30 April 1870
Place: Trimbakeshwar, Maharashtra
Death Date: 16 February 1944
Place: Nashik, Maharashtra

Life of Christ, a silent movie, was being screened in Bombay during Christmas in 1910. In the audience was a man who then dreamt of creating an indigenous film industry. He thought that the audience would be able to appreciate movies based on popular Indian legends. At a time when people hardly foresaw film-making as a commercial venture, he studied the art and achieved phenomenal breakthroughs to become a pioneer of the Indian film industry.

Dhundiraj Govind Phalke, popularly known as Dadasaheb Phalke, completed his studies in architecture and took up photography and landscape painting. When he realized his passion for film-making, he went on to learn the skills and discovered in himself a commendable string of talents. He was a painter, a photographer, a dramatics teacher, a printer, an engraver, and even a magician.

Phalke's illustrious career commenced with financial challenges. He found it difficult to raise funds and had to finally pledge his life's savings to travel abroad. He trained in film-making techniques and also purchased necessary equipment from England.

In 1913, he made *Raja Harishchandra*, India's first full-length film. It enjoyed instant success as thrilled audiences appreciated the portrayal of Indian legends on screen. Phalke went on to create other great works like *Mohini Bhasmasur* and *Satyavan Savitri*. Soon, the appeal of cinema displaced traditional entertainment mediums such as the theatre and the circus.

During his next visit to England, Phalke organized trade shows that were well-received. He returned to India with new equipment and continued film-making. He produced other successful films like *Lanka Dahan*, *Shri Krishna Janam* and *Kaliya Mardan* for which he received an overwhelming response. At a time when men enacted female roles, Phalke encouraged women to play women on screen, thus bringing them to a position of respect in the film industry.

As an exhibitor, Phalke travelled with his projector in bullock carts to showcase his films to rural audiences. He also established a model studio containing caves, fields, hills, forest and other picturesque landscape in the interiors. Technicians and artists lived on the premises, much like a family. He became famous for his special effects that were technically remarkable during those times.

A true visionary, Phalke made films offering wholesome mainstream entertainment during the silent era. His pioneering efforts attracted businessmen who realized the financial viability of film-making. During a career spanning nearly two decades, Phalke made twenty-six short films and 100 full-fledged movies. His last work *Gangavataran*, was filmed in 1937.

To commemorate the achievements of this pioneer of Indian film industry, the Dadasaheb Phalke Award was instituted in 1969. This annual award is one of the most coveted honours of Indian cinema. It comprises of a Swarna Kamal medallion, a shawl, and a cash prize, and is awarded only to great achievers as a recognition of their lifetime contribution to Indian cinema.

The Hockey Wizard

Name: Dhyan Chand Singh
Birth Date: 29 August 1905
Place: Allahabad, Uttar Pradesh
Death Date: 3 December 1979
Place: New Delhi

Dhyan Singh, a fourteen-year-old boy, was watching some army officers playing a hockey match in Jhansi. When the losing team was two goals behind target, he insisted on joining them. An officer granted him permission and Singh went to win the match by scoring four goals at an unbelievable pace. The officer predicted that this talented youngster would shine like the moon if he continued to play the game. Dhyan Singh came to be called Dhyan Chand Singh, *chand* meaning 'moon' in Hindi. A future hockey champion had been discovered.

Dhyan Chand's father served in the Indian Army and the family had to shift base quite often. This affected his studies and he could not continue his schooling after the sixth standard. In his younger years, Chand was inclined towards wrestling. At sixteen, he was inducted into the Punjab Regiment and received formal training in hockey. Dhyan Chand went on to deliver legendary performances in almost every tournament he participated in, demonstrating such impeccable dribbling skills that they resulted in the myth that he had magic in his hockey stick. The opposing team could never predict the fate of the game till the very end due to his uncanny ability to score goals. Soon, he became known as the 'Hockey Wizard'. Once, in Holland, officials even smashed his hockey stick to investigate whether there was a magnet inside.

The Indian team was victorious in almost every tournament he played as he single-handedly scored more than half the goals in every match. Don Bradman, the legendary cricketer, once remarked that Dhyan Chand scores goals like cricketers score runs. Dhyan Chand was instrumental in the Indian squad bagging gold medals at the Olympic Games in Amsterdam, Los Angeles and Berlin. He evolved into one of the greatest hockey players that the world had ever seen.

Dhyan Chand retired in 1948. The Dhyan Chand Tournament was initiated in his honour in 1951 at the National Stadium.

Goal, Dhyan Chand's autobiography, was published in 1952. He was the first hockey player to be awarded the Padma Bhushan in 1956. The same year, he retired from the Army as a major and, hence, is popularly referred to as Major Dhyan Chand. He later served as a coach for many years to the national team and trained budding players. Dhyan Chand's brother Roop Singh was also an acclaimed hockey player.

Though he would always set the field on fire, once off the field, Dhyan Chand chose to lead a quiet life. During his last years, he suffered from liver cancer.

Major Dhyan Chand's birthday, 29 August, is celebrated as National Sports Day in India. In 1979, the Government of India issued a postage stamp to honour this wizard of hockey. In 2002, the sports ministry introduced the Dhyan Chand Award, a lifetime achievement award for those legends who contribute not only during their illustrious sports careers but also after retiring.

Dhyan Chand still holds the record for being one of the greatest scorer of goals on the hockey field. He has secured a permanent place in the history of Indian sports by scoring over 1,000 goals in international tournaments.

The Enlightened One

Name: Gautama Buddha
Birth Date: 563 BC
Place: Lumbini, (now in Nepal)
Death (Nirvana): 483 BC
Place: Kushinagar, Uttar Pradesh

The Enlightened One lay on his deathbed. Anand, his disciple, tended to him and Bhadrak, a devotee, wept inconsolably. The Enlightened One asked, 'Anand, who is weeping?' Anand replied, 'It is Bhadrak. He is here to see you.'

'Then call him.'

Bhadrak fell at his feet and burst into loud sobs, saying, 'O Master, who shall now show us the light when you are gone?'

'Bhadrak, the light you seek is within you. Do not search for it in holy places, caves or forests. Those whose thoughts, speech and deeds are pure and in harmony, they find the light within their own selves. Be your own light!'

This was his last message to Bhadrak and to the world. Do you know who said these words? It was

Gautama Buddha, also known as Tathagata, and this message was his guiding motto.

Gautama Buddha was born as Siddhartha into a princely family in 563 BC in Lumbini near Kapilavastu in the foothills of Nepal. The royal family belonged to the Gautama gotra of the Sakya clan of the Suryavanshi race. His father was King Suddhodana and his mother was Queen Mahamaya, who unfortunately died soon after childbirth.

On the fifth day after his birth, wise men predicted that the newborn was destined to be either a monarch of the universe or a supreme enlightened being who would forsake worldly pleasures in search of knowledge. Unhappy to hear this, Suddhodana provided his son with all the luxuries and the best education within the palace so that Siddhartha would not be tempted to leave home at all, ever.

When Siddhartha was barely sixteen, Suddhodana got him married to Princess Yashodhara. In a few years, she bore him a son, Rahul. Soon after his son was born, Siddhartha began to feel restless and ventured out of the palace. For the first time, he saw the harsh realities of human life—a frail old man, a suffering and diseased man, a hungry beggar, a dead man—which made him realize that nothing in life is permanent. This sudden and acute awareness transformed his life.

Soon after, at the age of twenty-nine, Siddhartha left his palace quietly one night, without waking his wife and son. He roamed the country meeting saints and ascetics in his quest for inner peace and the Truth, but found neither.

One day, an exhausted Siddhartha wandered into Bodh Gaya and sat under a banyan tree to rest. He closed his eyes. Suddenly, he felt a divine light coming from within himself. He realized that the Truth is within every human being and it is futile to seek it outside of the Self. After this, Siddhartha came to be known as the Buddha, 'one who has woken up to reality'.

For the next four decades, till he attained *nirvana* at the age of eighty, the Buddha spread the message of spiritual life, laying emphasis on purification of mind, heart and soul. Known as 'the Middle Path', because it was midway between asceticism and indulgence, the Buddha's teaching was based on Four Noble Truths:

1. All human life is suffering.
2. All suffering is caused by human desire.
3. The end of human desire is the end of human suffering.
4. An end to all desire can be achieved by following the Noble Eightfold Path, which is that of right understanding, right thought, right action, right speech, right livelihood, right effort, right mindfulness, and right concentration.

Legend has it that a young woman once begged the Buddha to bring her dead child back to life. When the Buddha asked her to get a mustard seed from a home that had not suffered death, she visited every home only to realize that death is universal. She returned to the Buddha to learn the path that leads to eternal peace.

The Buddha's teachings are applicable even to the materialistic world of today. Some of his teachings are as follows: We are shaped by our thoughts. When the mind is pure, joy follows like a shadow that never leaves. You will not be punished for your anger but by your anger. Peace comes from within the Self. Virtue is persecuted more by the wicked than it is loved by the good. Hatred ceases only through love; this is the eternal rule.

On his deathbed, the Buddha is believed to have told his disciples not to follow any particular leader. Following the Buddha's parinirvana, the first Buddhist council was formed with Mahakasyapa as the first chairman of the Sangha.

The Buddha's teachings are popular all over the world. Buddhism, a religion largely based on the beliefs, practices, traditions and teachings of the Buddha, is the fourth largest religion practised in the world. Its two major braches are Theravada ('The School of the Elders') and Mahayana ('The Great Vehicle'). While Theravada is widespread in south-east Asia and Sri Lanka, Mahayana is popular in east Asia. Zen, Tibetan, Tiantai, Shinnyo-en and Nichiren Buddhism are part of Mahayana. Practices of individual schools vary but the foundation of the Buddhist tradition relies on the

Three Jewels: the Buddha, his teachings (*dharma*) and the community (*sangha*).

Wesak is an important festival celebrated by Buddhists on the full moon day in May. Also called Buddha Poornima, it marks the enlightenment and death of the Buddha. On this day, Buddhists chant, pray, decorate their homes, offer food, flowers and candles to monks and visit local temples for religious service. A popular ceremony on this day is 'Bathing the Buddha'—a ritual in which water is poured over the shoulders of an idol of the Buddha to show respect for the Buddha and his teachings. It also signifies purification of the mind from greed, hatred and ignorance.

The Founder of an Empire

Name: Ghanshyam Das Birla
Birth Date: 10 April 1894
Place: Pilani, Rajasthan
Death Date: 11 June 1983
Place: London, United Kingdom

This industrialist hailed from a traditional Marwari family of Pilani. When he took over the ancestral business of his grandfather Shiv Narayan Birla and his father Baldev Das Birla, he applied his own notions of diversification to inherited enterprise. After establishing two cotton mills, he shifted base to Calcutta along with his brother to enter into jute production. From a modest start—they lived in a single rented room— he went a long way to build a mammoth industrial empire at a time when business policies were in favour of European merchants.

Ghanshyam Das Birla's professional journey is quite remarkable. He had to overcome obstacles at almost every point of business expansion and diversification. Right from political and bureaucratic conflicts to lack of power to problems in acquiring licences, Birla faced it all. When Birla Jute Mills was established, it met with several challenges. However, he came out successful and then there was no looking back.

With a modest investment of fifty lakh rupees, the brothers started a mill in Gwalior and the Birla Brothers Ltd was established in 1919. Gradually, they diversified into many areas of business such as sugar, paper and cement, and within three decades, the brothers made it to the thirteenth slot among the largest managing agencies in India.

After being elected to the Central Legislative Assembly (British India) in 1926, G.D. Birla established the reputed Federation of Indian Chambers of Commerce and Industry (FICCI) in 1927, with the help of some other reputed industrialists.

The 1930s saw the development of paper and sugar mills by the Birla Group. However, his most successful venture is arguably the establishment of Hindustan Motors, which manufactured the iconic Ambassador car. It became synonymous with Indian households and enjoyed a monopoly on Indian roads for nearly three decades. In addition, he gave shape to one of the oldest commercial banks of India, United Commercial Bank, currently known as UCO Bank.

G.D. Birla also lent a strong and supportive hand to the Indian freedom movement and was a close friend and counsellor of Mahatma Gandhi. Apart from launching the influential newspaper the *Hindustan*

Times, he advised Gandhiji on various economic policies and supported the Indian National Congress in the pre-Independence era. Perhaps, on account of this association and Birla's faith in Gandhian philosophy, he declined the British offer of knighthood.

After Independence, he diversified into textiles and tea, apart from stepping into rayons, chemicals, cements as well as steel tubes.

Birla was a rebel, a man of eclectic business beliefs and well ahead of his contemporaries in his mental make-up. He could not conform to or compromise on aspects that he did not believe in. He believed that though money is easy to make, it is quite difficult to spend it optimally.

Birla disliked speculation and opted for profit without compromising on quality. His passion for work propelled him ahead. He was as interested in improving the efficiency of production in his sixties as he was in his younger years. Thus, irrespective of age, he directed his zeal and perseverance towards achieving excellence in work.

G.D. Birla was also famous for his philanthropic activities. A school dropout himself, he opened nearly 400 schools offering primary education. Ironically though, none of his children were graduates. He believed in pedigree more than meritorious certificates.

Birla dreamt of infrastructural development in his home town and founded the Birla Institute of Technology and Science, a centre for research and technical studies. The university had no faith in formal degrees like other colleges and came up with its own curriculum and teaching methods. Over the years, BITS, as it is now popularly called, has evolved into one of India's premier engineering institutions. Pilani also houses polytechnic colleges, residential schools and the famous Central Electrical and Electronics Research Institute.

G.D. Birla also established many hospitals, planetariums and temples popularly called Birla Mandirs. His grandfather's house, Birla Haveli, stands proud in Pilani, Rajasthan till today.

In 1957, he was conferred the Padma Vibhushan. The G.D. Birla Award for scientific research is given to budding scientists for their valuable contributions to scientific research.

The Birla group of industries was often compared with the Tata Group as their creative peaks were in the same period (1939–69). During this time, other corporate empires like Reliance and Bajaj also gradually emerged and went on to become success stories.

Having sowed the seeds of one of the largest and most diversified business groups of India, Birla has left a proud legacy and responsibility for his family. At least three contemporary business groups trace their ancestral roots to this dynamic and immortal legend.

Magician of the Flute

Name: Hariprasad Chaurasia
Birth Date: 1 July 1938
Place: Allahabad, Uttar Pradesh

Every morning, young Hariprasad would tell his father that he was going to the temple. However, he didn't really go there. Instead, he would go to a friend's house to practise singing for two hours, every day. Such focus, dedication and passion for music eventually led him to become the renowned Hariprasad Chaurasia, a flautist par excellence who has played his chosen instrument, the bansuri, at concerts across the world.

Hariprasad's mother died when he was very young. Along with his two siblings, he was raised by their father who was a professional wrestler and a disciplinarian. Hariprasad had to go for his music practice sessions surreptitiously because his father wanted his son to follow in his footsteps. Hariprasad was apprehensive that his father would punish him if he got to know of his musical pursuits. Fear did not, however, dampen his spirits. At the same time, to keep his father happy, he continued to pursue wrestling. He later acknowledged that his stamina and lung power had been developed due to his reluctant training as a wrestler.

At the age of nine, Hariprasad began learning vocal music under a guru named Pandit Rajaram, who also happened to be his neighbour. Of course, these lessons too happened in secrecy when his father was not around. Some years later, he started teaching children younger than himself to earn some pocket money.

When he was fifteen, Hariprasad heard the sound of a flute for the first time. The performance was being given by a flautist named Pandit Bholanath on All India Radio. Hariprasad fell in love with the sound. He landed up at Bholanath's residence and asked him for lessons.

Although Hariprasad was pretty sure that he wanted to make a career as a flautist, he started off by doing clerical work for the government. He later got a job at All India Radio in Orissa. While working there, he also began to be invited to perform at music recitals. Very often, he was asked to play the flute as an accompanying artist at Odissi dance recitals.

Soon he was transferred to Bombay where he got to know many film music directors. He quit his radio job and made a comfortable living working on music for films in collaboration with Pandit Shivkumar Sharma. However, making Bollywood music did not give him much creative satisfaction. He was earning well but not expanding his horizon as an artist. He realized that he could not be thus confined all his life. This is when he approached the reclusive sitar maestro Annapurna Devi to help him hone his skills in classical music. She was hard to convince; it took him three years to persuade her but, true to his character, he did not give up till she relented.

Thus began a new turn in Hariprasad's musical journey. Since Annapurna Devi was not a flautist, she taught him the notes by singing. Hariprasad attributes his achievement as a musician to her, and remains devoted to her, despite having become a seasoned artist in his own right.

Hariprasad is credited with popularizing the essentially earthy Indian folk instrument—the bamboo flute—and taking it to concert halls around the globe. He has played alongside many international artists including John McLaughlin and Jethro Tull. Some of his albums are *In A Mellow Mood*, *Call of the Valley*, *Basant Bahar*, and *Music Without Boundaries*.

Hariprasad Chaurasia has won many awards during his eventful career, including the Padma Bhushan, the Padma Vibhushan and the Sangeet Natak Academi Award. In 2009, the French government conferred on him the title Knight in the Order of Arts and Letters.

Chaurasia has been teaching Indian music at the Rotterdam Music Conservatory for two decades. Having acquired much fame, he is now also deeply committed to teaching his craft to many others through his music school Vrindavan in Odisha.

Says the maestro, 'In my dreams, I dream of recreating a huge college of flautists, a veritable Vrindavan in which students will arrive to learn and study with satchels full of flutes . . . A modern Vrindavan from which a thousand flutes will ring out everyday. For what else is there? When my breath is gone and I cannot play any more, what do I leave behind?'

Architect of Nuclear Science

Name: Homi Jehangir Bhabha
Birth Date: 30 October 1909
Place: Bombay, British India
Death Date: 24 January 1966
Place: Mont Blanc, France

No one can deny that India is a land richly blessed with intellectuals, a land where many research enthusiasts and academic scholars constantly strive for excellence. Their achievements have proved to be phenomenal and make for inspirational reading.

While some of them come from less privileged backgrounds, others have the advantage of being born in illustrious families and use their potential to the fullest with parental encouragement right from childhood. Such is the story of this brilliant scientist who shaped his interests in art and science with unflinching family support. Needless to mention, he was gifted with great aesthetic sense and abundant creativity as well as scientific aptitude.

Homi Bhabha was a hyperactive child and his parents were quite apprehensive whether he got adequate rest. They were relieved when the doctors certified that he was actually quite normal. His continuous flow of thoughts and superactive brain impelled him to develop a keen interest in science from an early age and he could grasp difficult theories with ease.

Bhabha loved books and owned a private library at home but he was not just a bookworm. Gifted with a creative brain, he also developed a love for art, nature, painting and literature. Some of his paintings now adorn art galleries in England.

An intelligent student, Bhabha won many prizes in his school days. After passing the Senior Cambridge Examination, he pursued engineering, to respect the wishes of his father and uncle. However, since his first love was physics, he decided to listen to his heart and convinced his father of his desire to pursue higher studies in the subject of his choice.

Time and again, Bhabha proved that Indian scientists were competent enough to gain international recognition. Ambitious yet practically oriented, he proved his mettle through efficient execution rather than mere theoretical speculation. He was a great planner and insisted on excellence in work. His research was original and he tirelessly invested time in a niche area where future results and the probability of success were uncertain.

Bhabha firmly believed in his innovative ideas and thoughts. In fact, he foresaw long ago that mankind would suffer due to complete dependence on fossil fuels to generate power. He believed that nuclear energy had great potential and would be a vital power source for the future. He also gave a whole new dimension to nuclear physics.

Bhabha was so passionate about his research that he turned down prestigious posts in order to concentrate on his work. A recipient of the prestigious Padma Bhushan, Bhabha is considered the 'Father of the Indian Atomic Energy Programme'. He discovered the famous Bhabha Scattering Effect and also spearheaded India's atomic energy programme for two decades. Utilizing his political connections and his own charisma, he established two major institutions, the Atomic Energy Commission and the Tata Institute of Fundamental Research.

Bhabha believed that a scientist belonged to the entire world, not to a particular nation. True to his ideals, he brought together talented young scientists who were interested in nuclear science on a common platform by arranging lectures.

This kind, helpful and gracious gentleman was a remarkable administrator and leader at work and yet attached deep importance to friendship. His closeness to Jawaharlal Nehru is well known. Bhabha loved dynamic individuals and forgave people who committed mistakes unknowingly, but never tolerated indifference, laziness or a careless attitude.

Bhabha dedicated his entire life to the world of physics and remained a bachelor all his life. When asked about matrimony, he quipped, 'I am married to creativity.' He died in a plane crash near Mont Blanc while travelling to attend a meeting. The Homi Bhabha Fellowship, instituted in his honour in 1967, is awarded to talented scientists for study and research.

The Iron Lady of India

Name: Indira Priyadarshini Gandhi
Birth Date: 19 November 1917
Place: Allahabad, Uttar Pradesh
Death Date: 31 October 1984
Place: New Delhi

A fourteen-year-old girl asked her ailing mother, 'Who will look after Father when you are no more?' Her mother answered, 'He will be your responsibility.' The girl asked, 'But who will look after him when I get married and have a family of my own?' The mother replied, 'A woman is a mother to one and all.'

The girl was Indira, the mother Kamala Nehru. Following her mother's advice, Indira not only took care of her father but also shouldered the mammoth task of looking after the concerns of India as a whole.

Born into a family of influential national leaders, Indira was the only child of Kamala and Jawaharlal Nehru, who eventually became the first prime minister of independent India. She was also deeply influenced by Gandhiji who frequently visited their household.

Since her childhood, Indira was very fond of reading.

She was also highly inspired by Joan of Arc and the tale of her martyrdom. When a teacher in school asked little Indira what she would like to be when she grew up, the teacher expected an answer that kids of her age usually came up with—a teacher or a doctor or a lawyer. Indira surprised her with her reply: 'I would like to be someone like Joan of Arc.'

Indira's journey on the road to power and politics started when she turned twelve. She became the leader of a children's group in Allahabad called the Monkey Brigade, whose objective was to help end British control over India. Indira delivered speeches while the other members safeguarded Congress workers by forewarning them of imminent arrests or house raids by the British.

After finishing school, Indira joined Santiniketan, an educational institution set up by Rabindranath Tagore. It was Tagore who gave her the name 'Priyadarshini'.

Indira Priyadarshini went to England for higher studies. While studying at Somerville College, University of Oxford, she became a member of the radical pro-independence London-based India League. This was not only her initiation into active politics but also the time when she met Feroze Gandhi, her future husband.

Indira also spent some time in Switzerland where her mother relocated due to ill health. Kamala Nehru passed away in 1936 and Indira returned to India two years later to join the Indian National Congress. She married Feroze Gandhi in 1942 and, soon after, the two of them were imprisoned by the British at Naini Central Jail in Allahabad on charges of subversion. They remained in custody until 13 May 1943.

India gained independence from the British in 1947. Jawaharlal Nehru became free India's first prime minister. Indira's interests were entrenched in politics by now. She was her father's constant companion, both as a hostess and confidante, despite having a family of her own. After her father's death, she became a member of parliament and served in the cabinet as the minister for information and broadcasting.

Due to the then prime minister Dr Lal Bahadur Shastri's sudden death, Indira Priyadarshini Gandhi became the automatic choice for the nation's leadership. In 1967, she became the first woman ever elected to lead a democracy. She was re-elected in 1971 for another term. The campaign slogan that ensured her victory was *Garibi Hatao* ('Abolish Poverty').

Indira's achievements as prime minister of India were as follows:

- India won the war against Pakistan in 1971 and Bangladesh was created.
- She and Pakistan President Zulfikar Ali Bhutto signed the Shimla Agreement, which bound the two countries to resolve the Kashmir dispute through peaceful means and negotiations.
- To boost trade, India decreed a 40 per cent

devaluation of the Indian rupee from 4 to 7 to the US dollar.

- A national nuclear programme was launched in 1967 in response to a nuclear threat from China. India conducted a successful underground nuclear test, unofficially called 'Smiling Buddha', at Pokhran. India became the world's youngest nuclear power.

- Her support to the Green and White Revolutions— special agriculture and dairy innovation programmes—transformed India's chronic food shortage into surplus production and resulted in the nation exporting wheat, rice, cotton and milk.

However, people were not happy with the high inflation, rampant corruption and poor living standards of the time, and this catalysed general unrest. Indira's downfall began when she recommended that President Fakhruddin Ali Ahmed declare a state of emergency to contain the unrest. In 1977, she called for fresh elections but lost miserably. However, she returned to power in 1980.

In 1984, she ordered Operation Blue Star, an assault on the Golden Temple in Amritsar, to crush the secessionist movement of Sikh militants led by Bhindranwale. These militants were holed up in the Temple. Bhindranwale and several other militants were killed, and the Temple was damaged. The Sikh community bitterly resented her action, which was seen as desecration of their sacred place of worship. In a most vengeful act, two of her personal bodyguards assassinated Indira on 31 October 1984.

A skilled and intelligent politician, Indira acquired a formidable reputation as a statesperson, both in India and across the world. She believed that 'A nation's strength ultimately consists in what it can do on its own, not in what it can borrow from others.'

Her legacy continues. Over twenty-five years after her death, the Congress Party is still in power. As the world's longest serving female prime minister, Indira Gandhi remains an icon of empowerment for Indian women.

Chacha Nehru

Name: Jawaharlal Nehru
Birth Date: 14 November 1889
Place: Allahabad, United Provinces, British India
Death Date: 27 May 1964
Place: New Delhi

This favourite disciple of Mahatma Gandhi is also considered the architect of modern India. A highly influential leader of the Indian freedom struggle, he was also elected as the leader of the Congress party due to his firm principles, conviction and ideals. He took part in the challenging negotiations for the India–Pakistan Partition and, after Independence, became the first prime minister of Independent India, hoisted the national flag, gave a memorable speech from the ramparts of the Red Fort, and held the post for the longest tenure in Indian history.

Nehru was determined to build an economically and socially stable nation. He launched a series of initiatives and forged strong alliances with foreign countries. He founded institutional democracy in India and carved out major policies to support it. The blueprints of parliamentary democracy and judiciary, armed forces and civil service, fundamental principles like secularism, equality, and social justice were all drafted with major contributions from him.

Nehru was also responsible for establishing the Planning Commission of India and was involved in the first three Five-Year Plans that the commission drafted. He believed in stabilizing inter-state relationships and envisioned that modernization and development of science and technology is the key to achieve economic development.

Jawaharlal Nehru was born to Motilal Nehru and Swaroop Rani. He had quite a modern upbringing and received elite education in some of the finest schools and colleges across the world. The family was well ahead of its contemporaries. He was taught at home by Scottish and English teachers. Nehru's exposure widened during his education and stay in England, which also kindled his patriotism. He returned to India in 1912 and initially practised law.

Influenced by Gandhi's principles and teachings, the entire Nehru family abandoned expensive pastimes and possessions. Nehru would wear khadi and a Gandhi cap, and was known for the rose in his buttonhole. He was deeply engaged in the freedom struggle and was arrested and imprisoned multiple times. During his tenure as president of the Allahabad Municipal Corporation, he established various educational institutions and also worked on the development of sanitation and health care.

Nehru married Kamala Kaul in 1916. Kamala, who hailed from a traditional background, was initially intimidated by the unconventional Nehru family. However, she was a devoted wife and supported Nehru in his pursuits. In fact, during the Non-Cooperation Movement, she teamed up with other dynamic women and picketed shops that sold foreign goods and liquor.

The couple had one daughter, Indira Priyadarshini. She later came to be known as Indira Gandhi after her marriage to Feroze Gandhi. In 1955, Nehru was deservedly conferred the Bharat Ratna. Fondly called 'Chacha Nehru' by children, his birthday on 14 November is celebrated as National Children's Day.

Nehru was a gifted writer and authored several books, such as *The Discovery of India*, *Glimpses of World History* and his autobiography entitled *Toward Freedom*.

Through his long and chequered political journey, Nehru has left a proud legacy that is being effectively carried forward by his future generations. Nehru's daughter Indira and grandson Rajiv Gandhi both served as India's prime ministers. There is also a reputed university set up in his honour in Delhi. Nehru planetariums are scattered across the country. Nehru's former residence at Teen Murti House now contains a world-class library and museum.

Industrialist Par Excellence

Name: Jehangir Ratanji Dadabhoy (JRD) Tata
Birth Date: 29 July 1904
Place: Paris, France
Death Date: 29 November 1993
Place: Geneva, Switzerland

Jehangir Ratanji Dadabhoy Tata or JRD was the son of Ratanji Dadabhoy Tata and his French wife, Sooni. The couple had five children. On 29 July 1904, when their second child was born in Paris, they gave him the Persian name Jehangir meaning 'conqueror of the world'.

After being educated in France, Japan and England, JRD was drafted into the French army for a mandatory one-year period. After army service, JRD was keen to secure an engineering degree from Cambridge but his father summoned him to India. At the age of twenty-one, in December 1925, JRD was inducted into the House of Tatas, the family business, as an unpaid apprentice.

The very next year, Ratanji passed away. Jehangir inherited his father's position as a permanent director of Tata Sons, the group's flagship company. In 1929, he surrendered his French citizenship and became a citizen of India.

In the same year, JRD received his flying licence, which bore on it the number one, a position that he was soon to rise to in the Indian industry. Jehangir's passion for flying was fulfilled with the formation of the Tata Aviation Service in 1932. On 15 October 1932, the first flight of Indian civil aviation took off from Karachi with the adventurous JRD at the controls of a Puss Moth, flying solo to Bombay. In 1946, Tata Airlines, a division of Tata Sons, became a full-fledged company called Air India, which continues to serve India as one of its leading airlines.

At the young age of thirty-four, JRD became the fourth chairman of Tata Group, India's largest industrial empire. JRD is credited with placing the group on the international map. Under his leadership, in half a century, Tata Sons grew from a group of fourteen enterprises to a conglomerate of ninety-five—from airlines to hotels, trucks to locomotives, chemicals and pharmaceuticals to financial services, tea and air conditioning to cologne and cosmetics.

However, JRD gave himself credit only for the establishment of Air India. For the other accomplishments, he acknowledged the contribution of his executives. Such was the philosophy he developed and maintained in the Tata Group—only merit counts. His professionalism showed in both the quality of the products he strove to deliver, as well as, in the positive work culture he aimed at creating within the industry. With over sixty years of experience in top management, he developed his own philosophy and method where leadership was concerned. He once spoke of how he brought out the best in people: 'At times, it involved suppressing yourself. It is painful but necessary . . . To lead men, you have to lead them with affection.'

JRD stepped down from his position as chairman in 1991, handing over the baton to Ratan Tata.

In 1982, he retraced his historic flight from Karachi to Bombay to mark the golden jubilee of Indian civil aviation.

JRD Tata was honoured with numerous awards, including the Padma Vibhushan in 1957, the Guggenheim Medal for aviation in 1988 and India's highest civilian honour, the Bharat Ratna, in 1992. He also received the Legion of Honour from the French government.

JRD and his wife Thelma did not have any children, but he always appeared to be comfortable and at ease with kids. In fact, be it children or adults, it was people who mattered to him.

JRD passed away in 1993 in a Geneva hospital. He is interred at Père Lachaise Cemetery in Paris.

The Mystic Poet

Name: Kabir Das
Period: AD 1440–1518

Despite not receiving any formal education, this revered saint is considered to be one of the most extraordinary poet-mystics of India. His teachings deeply influenced both the Bhakti and the Sufi movements. He also contributed almost 500 powerful verses to the Sikhs' holy scripture, Sri Guru Granth Sahib.

Kabir's *dohas* ('couplets') explain ethical values and principles through simple examples picked from day-to-day life. One can relate to these verses at a spiritual as well as a practical level. To this date, Kabir's *dohas* are admired and used by people, irrespective of religious background. He has attracted followers from all walks of life with his fearless preaching and his easily-understood philosophy about life.

Sant Kabir was a social reformer and a staunch believer in the equality of human beings. He opposed the caste system and the associated social hierarchy. He believed in the existence of the Almighty and in surrendering to the supreme power that controls every sphere of existence. According to him, salvation could be achieved by the union of the *jivatma* ('personal soul') with *paramatma* ('the Almighty'). His affinity towards and respect for Vaishnavism, Vedanta and Sufism in addition to the Nath Yogi teachings are reflected in his compositions

There are various legends surrounding Kabir's birth. Some believe that he was abandoned as an infant by a Brahmin widow and discovered floating on a lotus leaf by a Muslim weaver from Benaras.

Inclined towards spirituality from a very young age, Kabir wanted to become a disciple of the great Vaishnava saint Ramanand. When his religion came in the way, he played a simple trick to achieve his goal. Ramanand visited a bathing ghat every morning and, one day, Kabir intentionally came under Ramanand's feet. Ramanand was shocked and chanted 'Rama! Rama!' At this point, Kabir pleaded with the saint to accept him as a disciple. Ramanand was impressed by Kabir's appeal and happily granted his desires.

Interestingly, Kabir did not renounce the world to profess his teachings. A weaver by occupation, he successfully balanced his life as a mystic as well as his responsibilities as a householder.

Kabir advocated ahimsa, protested against animal slaughter and was a vegetarian.

Kabir faced many conflicts in his lifetime, as he had been brought up by a Muslim but was taught by a Hindu guru. He was initially ridiculed when he preached in order to change the mindset of the people from the lower strata of society. Kabir's teachings represented a fusion of Hindu and Muslim tenets. From Hinduism, he picked up the concept of reincarnation and the law of karma. From Islam, he accepted the affirmation of a single god and the rejection of both idol worship and the caste system. By combining aspects from diverse religions, he won the hearts of millions during his lifetime.

Legend goes that when Kabir passed away, a tomb as well as a temple was constructed in his memory. The legacy of Kabir is carried forward by his followers. Estimated to be more than ninety-six lakh spread all over the world, they form the religious community named Kabir Panth.

Shining Star

Name: Kalpana Chawla
Birth Date: 1 July 1961
Place: Karnal, Haryana
Death Date: 1 February 2003
Place: Over Texas

This ordinary girl, who hailed from a modest family, dreamt of stars, sky and space—and also managed to reach them in her lifetime!

Fondly called Montu by her loving and supportive family, she holds the distinction of being the first Indian woman astronaut to enter space in 1997. Unfortunately, her second space expedition claimed her life as she was one of the victims of the Space Shuttle Columbia disaster on 1 February 2003.

The entire world was awaiting the descent of this space shuttle at Florida after its twenty-eighth mission, poised to celebrate the happy occasion of the successful return of its crew members. Newspapers flashed the exact minute that they could salute the heroes as the space shuttle flew past their respective countries.

No one had ever dreamt that it would end as a night of grief and mourning. The shuttle unexpectedly disintegrated over Texas, leaving the world in a state of shocked disbelief.

Kalpana had developed a keen interest in space and in flying from a very young age. A brilliant student at school, she made numerous sketches and models of the space, sky, stars and planets. She was inspired by J.R.D. Tata, one of India's top industrialists and an aviation pioneer. As a child, she found it exciting to ride in Pushpak planes at Karnal's flying club.

Despite her father's opposition, Kalpana pursued her Bachelors in aeronautical engineering, the only female student in her batch. Later, she completed her Masters as well as her doctorate in the US, encouraged by her husband Jean-Pierre Harrison, an aviation writer and flying instructor himself. Kalpana became a US citizen in 1990. She was also a certified flight instructor for gliders and airplanes and held commercial pilot licences for gliders, seaplanes and single and multi-engine airplanes.

Kalpana applied to NASA in 1994 but had apprehensions about getting selected as she was too short to work in a space station. The white uniform that astronauts had to wear when being transferred from the shuttle to the space station did not fit her. Hence, she was restricted to duties inside the space shuttle.

After her first expedition in 1997, Kalpana fondly recalled the Himalayas, the Ganges valley and the Nile River as the most spectacular landmarks of the world.

Apart from flying, Kalpana loved to go hiking and backpacking. Her physical fitness, mental agility and wide experience qualified her for a second space expedition. She carried with her a silk banner dedicated to her favourite teacher, Nirmala Namboothiripad.

Sadly, her last visit to India had been more than a decade before her second expedition. When the news about the disaster was flashed, her family was devastated and at a loss for words.

Kalpana's brother Sanjay once said, 'To me, my sister is not dead. She is immortal. Isn't that what a star is? She is a permanent star in the sky. She will always be up there where she belongs.'

After her tragic death, NASA posthumously awarded Kalpana Chawla a medal for her distinguished service to the organization. In fact, a supercomputer is also named after her, as is an asteroid. Steve Morse from Kalpana's favourite band Deep Purple composed a song titled *Contact Lost* in memory of the Columbia disaster. Hospitals, hostels and scholarships have been set up in Kalpana's memory to keep her inspirational story alive for generations to come.

The Haryana Hurricane

Name: Kapil Dev Ramlal Nikhanj
Birth Date: 6 January 1959
Place: Chandigarh

It was 25 June 1983, a Saturday. People all over the cricket-loving world were glued to their television sets to watch the World Cup Final between West Indies and India. Much to the disappointment of Indian spectators, the sky was overcast and the Indians had managed an unimpressive score of 183 runs. It looked like it was all over for the Indian squad. But what followed at Lords Cricket Ground, London, was completely unexpected. It turned out to be one of the most upsetting defeats for the West Indies and a fabulous innings for the Indians. The finals of the 1983 World Cup saw the West Indies fall flat at 140 runs and the proud Indian captain lifted the trophy to the skies!

Kapil Dev's successful captaincy claimed global recognition and also gained respect for India by establishing her potential in cricket. In addition, fast-paced One-Day International (ODI) matches became more popular than long-drawn Test matches. Kapil had already gained 250 wickets in Test matches and was still going strong. Everybody looked forward to his prolific performances and expected him to scale higher peaks of achievements.

In 1984, Kapil suffered a severe knee injury that seriously impacted his bowling ability. However, he never lost his fitness, stamina or willpower during this challenging period and continued playing Test matches as well as ODIs. In 1992, he became the second cricketer in the world after Richard Hadlee to cross the 400-wicket mark.

The seeds of inspiration were sown when he was just fifteen, and part of the Under-19 League. After the rigorous practice sessions, the team was served dry chapattis and steamed vegetables. Kapil, who had a healthy appetite, claimed that he required adequate food to acquire the stamina for fast bowling. He felt deeply humiliated in front of his team when an official of the cricket board told him, 'There are no fast bowlers in India.' This moved Kapil to tears and he resolved to become the best pace bowler that India had ever produced. He went on to score 1,000 runs and take 100 wickets by the time he turned twenty, within a year and a half of joining the team.

Fondly called the Haryana Hurricane, Kapil also proved to be destructive batsman who could unsettle bowlers with his stroke play. In a Test, at Lords, he hit four sixes in succession, surprising the spectators who applauded his entertaining innings. Indeed, Kapil was one of the greatest all-rounders of his time. He often stabilized a game by batting in the last ten overs, when the pressure on the batsmen is the highest if the target is out of reach. In 1992, he played in his last World Cup and, after becoming the highest wicket taker for India in Tests (434 wickets), he announced his retirement in 1994.

Kapil's exemplary skills as a player and a captain earned him the challenging position of India's national cricket coach in September 1999. While the team tasted success during the first Test series at home against New Zealand, the subsequent eight Tests ended up in losses. Besides, the squad won just nine ODIs out of the twenty-five they played. Further, Kapil was charged with match-fixing, for which he received tremendous flak from all over. As a result, less than a year after becoming coach, Kapil resigned. Though allegations of his involvement in match-fixing were later proved to be false, Kapil could not come to terms with the manner in which the issue had been dealt with.

In 2000, he became the only Asian Founding Member of the Laureus Foundation. Based in Switzerland, the foundation works to promote sports and support economically and socially deprived youths. Kapil chose to stay away from the media glare until he was lauded as Wisden Indian Cricketer of the Century in 2002. He later contributed as a bowling consultant and was nominated as chairman of the National Cricket Academy (NCA) in 2006. In 2007, when Kapil Dev was appointed to the board of the Indian Cricket League (ICL) established by Zee Entertainment Enterprises, the Board of Control for Cricket in India perceived it as a conflict of interest and removed him from the post of NCA chairman.

Kapil married Romi Bhatia in 1980, and their daughter Amiya Dev was born sixteen years later. Kapil likes to play golf, a game he took up after his retirement in 1994.

He has published three autobiographical works: *By God's Decree*, *Cricket, My Style* and *Straight from the Heart*. He has made special appearances in Bollywood movies like *Iqbal* and *Mujhse Shaadi Karogi*. He owns restaurants called Kapils Eleven and Kaptains Retreat in Patna and Chandigarh. Partnering with Musco Lighting, he has also started Dev Musco Lighting Private Ltd to install floodlights in major sports venues and stadiums in India. He has also endorsed several leading brands.

By the end of his career, Kapil had taken over 400 wickets and scored over 4,000 runs in Test matches. He is deservedly the proud recipient of the Padma Shri, the Padma Bhushan and the Arjuna Award among other prestigious honours.

Kapil is synonymous with the game of cricket. He will always be remembered for his uncomplicated and intelligent approach to the game as a batsman, bowler, fielder, and captain who made India proud by clinching the glorious win in 1983. In 2010, Kapil was inducted into the ICC Cricket Hall of Fame.

Magician of the Pen

Name: Khushwant Singh
Birth Date: 2 February 1915
Place: Hadali, British India

The famous proverb goes: 'The pen is mightier than the sword.' For some, even scribbling can become a work of magic.

This powerful writer was teaching in the US when he received an offer to take over a popular Indian magazine called the *Illustrated Weekly of India*. He was in his fifties then. His potential had been recognized only from his contributions to various Indian and international journals. Thus, a relative novice in the field of journalism with no proven track record in editing and publishing was all set to make a flying start in a new arena supported only by his phenomenal ability to write. And once he stepped in, there was no looking back, either for the journal (until he served his tenure) or for him (as a journalist and writer). This magician wielding the pen is Khushwant Singh.

Khushwant adopted a completely revolutionary approach to revamping the periodical. He ensured that the *Weekly* became reader-centric, looked elegant, and dealt with subjects of topical relevance as wide-ranging as politics, economics, religion and art. The magazine became a rage across India. Within a year of his taking over, the circulation shot up rapidly from a mere 60,000 copies to over four lakh copies, which were sold out as soon as they hit the stands.

Another significant contribution by Khushwant to the world of journalism is his weekly column series titled 'With Malice towards One and All' in the *Hindustan Times*. Contrary to its name, it comprises articles reflecting complete secularism coupled with messages spreading peace. Occupying two full-length columns on the editorial page of the Saturday edition, it included essays, travelogues, and commentaries on culture, literature, political and socio-economic events. His witty punch-lines that compared conflicts in the socio-cultural behaviour of westerners and Indians were a major hit among his fans. The column also included contributions from readers (snippets or jokes) to encourage writing among people.

Khushwant was the editor of *Yojana*, an Indian government journal, and two leading newspapers in India, *Hindustan Times* and *National Herald*. The main reason behind his stupendous success was his dedication and personal involvement in his work. He personally edited all the drafts and often rewrote articles, giving them a completely new direction. He was known to wake up as early as 4 a.m. to write his columns in hand. His hard work paid off as the response he received from his loyal readers was phenomenal.

Writing comes naturally to this gifted personality. Khushwant understands the pulse of his readers very well and infuses energy and flavour into his contemporary articles by giving people exactly what they want—information, amusement and food for thought.

Khushwant has never restricted his talent to a particular writing style. He can present anything from scientific explanations to interesting trivia. His translations of religious texts and Urdu poetry are outstanding. His content is simple, straightforward and, more importantly, honest. His witty and refreshing style captures the reader's attention with ease. Khushwant never fears admitting his mistakes, weaknesses or even his failing health recently. No wonder he was chosen as the 'Honest Man of the Year' by Sulabh International in 2000.

Writing brought him not only fame but also controversies. Yet he boldly used his journalistic skill as a tool to bring about many positive changes across the nation. For instance, hunting was banned in many states thanks to his direct interaction with politicians. He also personally contributed through his powerful writings during the Bangladesh war. Controversies surfaced now and then but this dynamic man continued his work, as he was convinced about the transformation he wanted to bring about through the fine strokes of his magical pen.

Khushwant has written about thirty books and nearly half a dozen short stories. The author of the bestseller *Train To Pakistan* is also the recipient of Padma Bhushan and Padma Vibhushan. Other important honours include Punjab Rattan Award, Sahitya Akademi Fellowship Award and the Rockefeller Grant.

Even in his nineties, Khushwant attracts a huge fan following. An adolescent at heart, he is agile and active as ever and finds it difficult to sit still or relax. Even today, he records in his notebook every single magical word that fleets by.

An Icon of Heroism

Name: Kiran Bedi
Birth Date: 9 June 1949
Place: Amritsar, Punjab

During the early 1980s, as India prepared for the Asian Games to be held in Delhi, traffic conditions in the capital were quite chaotic. The numerous sports stadiums and flyovers under construction for the sports meet added to the chaos, causing roadblocks and traffic jams. The system fostered unruliness and bribery and threatened to smash the reputation of the city police.

A certain officer—the then deputy commissioner of police (chief of traffic) and the first woman in the Indian police force—took up the challenge of controlling the confusing scenario. She worked nineteen hours a day, standing on the streets herself to ensure implementation of laws. She increased commuter awareness, enforced fines, and indiscriminately towed away all vehicles parked outside designated areas.

The highlight of the goings-on was when a sub-inspector in her unit hauled away the then Prime Minister Indira Gandhi's official car, which had been parked in an unauthorized area for repairs. The superior in question staunchly supported her subordinate when the heat was turned on him in an enquiry. The police officer was Dr Kiran Bedi, and this incident earned her the nickname 'Crane' Bedi.

Kiran was born in Amritsar, the second of four daughters of Prem Lata and Prakash Lal Peshawaria. She attended Sacred Heart Convent School, where she joined the National Cadet Corps. She also took up tennis, a passion she inherited from her father, and won several championships like the All-India Interstate Women's Lawn Tennis Championship in the 1970s and also the Asian Ladies Title, when she was twenty-two years old. She studied English literature at Government College for Women, Amritsar, and earned her Masters in political science from Punjab University, Chandigarh, graduating at the top of her class.

Her urge to do outstanding work drew her to the police force. In July 1972, she gave up her lectureship at Khalsa College for Women to join the Indian Police Service. While in active service, she continued her educational pursuits and obtained a law degree in 1988 as well as a doctorate in social sciences in 1993.

During her tenure with the police, Kiran influenced several important decisions of the police service in the areas of narcotics control, traffic management and VIP security. As inspector general of prisons, at Tihar Jail in Delhi, she instituted several reforms in jail administration as well as prisoner care. For this, she was awarded the Ramon Magsaysay Award in 1994. She has also received several other honours, including the President's Gallantry Award (1979), Asia Region Award for Drug Prevention and Control (1991), Father Machismo Humanitarian Award (1995),) and Mother Teresa Memorial National Award for Social Justice (2005).

Kiran also worked with the United Nations in New York as police advisor to the secretary general. She served as India's representative to several international forums on crime prevention, drug abuse, police and prison reforms and women's issues. After taking voluntary retirement in the year 2007, Kiran launched a website, www.saferindia.com. Its motto is to help people whose complaints are not accepted by the local police. She has founded two non-profit, voluntary NGOs, India Vision Foundation and Navjyoti, for community development.

Kiran has hosted a TV show called *Aap Ki Kachehri, Kiran Ke Saath*. Her biography was the subject of an Australian non-fiction feature film called *Yes Madame, Sir*. It won several awards. Recently, she has been actively engaged with the fight against corruption and the movement to gather public support for the Jan Lokpal Bill.

Kiran Bedi has shown how even a single willing individual can make a difference to the country. She is a national icon who has made her mark and shown the way to many others.

Biotech Queen of India

Name: Kiran Mazumdar Shaw
Birth Date: 23 March 1953
Place: Bangalore, Karnataka

Kiran Mazumdar Shaw's life story is quite similar to the fables told to youngsters to motivate them to realize their dreams. She had humble origins but went on to achieve the heights of success, which only a chosen few can attain.

Kiran's father was a brewer for the India-based United Breweries. Kiran has confessed on numerous occasions that as a student at Bishop Cotton Girls' School, she was deeply embarrassed by the fact that her father worked for the liquor industry. She felt it was a tainted profession. One day, she spoke to him about how this sense of shame had been troubling her. He heard her out and then clarified that brewing was a science, not simply a matter of getting drunk. He added: 'Do not judge things, people and issues with incomplete information. There is truth in everything you see around you. So look for everything in its entirety.'

This, Kiran admits, became the basis of her life's philosophy. She graduated with honours in zoology from Bangalore University in 1973. She could have continued with zoology or genetics but she wanted to study a branch related to industrial applications. So she went to Ballarat College in Melbourne, Australia, to specialize in malting and brewing technology. However, on her return to India, she found that no company was willing to offer a job in brewing to a woman.

Her inability to pursue a career in brewing propelled her into the then new field of biotechnology. She joined as a trainee manager with Biocon Biochemicals Ltd. Impressed by her drive and ambition, Leslie Auchincloss, the owner of Biocon, offered her a partnership in a new venture to extract enzymes for alcoholic beverages, paper and other products. That was when Biocon India shot into India's industrial scenario.

Kiran started Biocon India in 1978 in the garage of her rented house in Bangalore with a meagre capital of 10,000 rupees. She faced funding problems because biotech was a new field and banks were not yet ready to invest in the enterprise. She also faced challenges because she was a woman entrepreneur, a rare breed. There were technological challenges as well, since India did not have the infrastructure for a biotech business. Kiran surmounted all these challenges and Biocon India became the first Indian company to manufacture and export enzymes to US and Europe.

Kiran says, 'If you have a vision, no matter how big or small, a plan, no matter if it is imperfect, but if there is passion and conviction for it, success is inevitable.'

The company expanded rapidly and its stock market value skyrocketed to such dizzy heights that Kiran, with nearly 40 per cent stake in the company, became India's richest businesswoman, worth 2,100 crore rupees. Today, Biocon India is one of the leading biotech companies in the world and the seventh largest biotech employer in the world. It also has the largest insulin and statin producing facilities in Asia.

Apart from setting up Biocon India, Kiran's contributions to social services are exemplary. She started the Biocon Foundation to conduct education, health and sanitation programmes for the benefit of the economically weaker sections of society. The foundation conducts free health care camps and provides mobile medical services. In 2007, she helped establish the 1,400-bed Mazumdar Shaw Cancer Centre at Bommasandra, Bangalore, along with Dr Devi Shetty. Coincidentally, her husband John Shaw is himself battling kidney cancer.

Along this awe-inspiring journey of continuous success, Kiran has been honoured with many prestigious titles and awards, including the Rotary Award for Best Model Employer in 1983, the Ernst & Young Entrepreneur of the Year award (health care and life sciences) in 2002, the Businesswoman of the Year award from the *Economic Times*, a lifetime achievement award from the Indian Chamber of Commerce in 2005, and the Wharton Infosys Business Transformation Award in 2006. The Government of India has conferred on her the prestigious Padma Shri (1989) and Padma Bhushan (2005).

What sets Kiran apart is her deep sense of integrity, along with her penchant for honesty and justice. Her motto—'succeeding against all odds'—propels her to achieve the goals she sets for herself.

The Dynamic Astrophysicist

Name: Krishnaswamy Kasturirangan
Birth Date: 24 October 1940
Place: Ernakulam, Kerala

India has earned global recognition in the field of space exploration and research, thanks to the tremendous advancements achieved in these areas in recent decades. From its modest beginning where scientists manually built electronic circuitry, the Indian space programme has now become a large, integrated, self-reliant unit capable of building world-class satellites as well as launching space vehicles.

The credit for these commendable developments goes largely to the dynamic chairman of the Indian Space Research Organization, ISRO, who brilliantly guided the space programme during its trying times and helped it achieve numerous milestones during its evolution. From developing remote sensing satellites and communication satellites in addition to the Polar Satellite Launch Vehicle (PSLV) as well as the Geo

Synchronous Satellite Launch Vehicle (GSLV), India has successfully established its expertise in diverse areas of space research and exploration under the leadership of Dr Krishnaswamy Kasturirangan.

After graduating from Bombay University in 1961 and completing his Masters in 1963, he received his doctorate for experimental high energy astronomy while working at the Physical Research Laboratory, Ahmedabad, in 1971. Dr Kasturirangan was initially the director of the ISRO Satellite Centre, where he oversaw the development of some popular new-generation satellites, like the INSAT series and remote sensing satellites.

Dr Kasturirangan led the prestigious Bhaskara projects, India's first step into experimenting with earth observation satellites. The development of Chandrayaan, India's first unmanned lunar probe, marked the beginning of planetary exploration measures by India, making it one of the six major countries to invest in major space initiatives.

ISRO gradually attained success after overcoming challenging obstacles in its experimental stages. But this visionary had the confidence and perseverance to streamline the critical processes and operations. Ably assisted by his team of research scientists and space experts, he gradually compelled global leaders to turn towards India for expertise.

As an astrophysicist, Dr Kasturirangan was also interested in X-ray as well as Gamma ray astronomy.

The ambitious high energy astronomy observatory established under his leadership has contributed immensely to the study and effects of cosmic X-rays as well as the Gamma rays in the lower strata of the atmosphere.

Dr Kasturirangan has published over 200 papers in both Indian and international journals in the areas of space science and astronomy. He has also been awarded honorary doctorates by almost sixteen universities. In addition to his famous convocation addresses at various universities, Dr Kasturirangan has delivered over 300 lectures at several educational institutions across the globe.

During his stint of thirty-five years in the Department of Space, Dr Kasturirangan was conferred three civilian honours from the Indian Government—Padma Vibhushan, Padma Bhushan and Padma Shri. After a brief tenure as a member of the Rajya Sabha, he is now a member of the Planning Commission of India, the chancellor of Jawaharlal Nehru University and also the director of the National Institute of Advanced Studies, Bangalore.

The Violin Maestro

Name: Lakshminarayana Subramaniam
Birth Date: 23 July 1947
Place: Madras, Tamil Nadu

This senior violinist is not only a talented performer but also a prolific organizer and composer of both Western and Indian classical music. Apart from his evergreen solo compositions, he has made over 200 recordings in collaboration with international musical maestros such as Yehudi Menuhin. This versatile musician has also accompanied many reputed Carnatic vocalists and classical musicians in their concerts.

L. Subramaniam hailed from a musically inclined Tamil family and gave his first performance at the age of six. Though he chose to study medicine, he was inspired by his parents to opt for music as his profession. Very soon, he established his mastery over the violin and was bestowed with the title of 'Violin Chakravarthy'.

Taking advantage of his strong foundation in different musical genres, Subramaniam created the concept of global music. In his breakthrough composition titled

Global Fusion, he brought together artists from five continents. Some of his other masterpieces include *Turbulence, Spring–Rhapsody, The Concert of Two Violins, Global Symphony Double Concerto for Violin and Flute*, and *Fantasy on Vedic Chants*. His emotive playing, unusual musical interpretation and readiness to experiment and improvise has attracted maestros from across the world to collaborate with him.

Reputed dance companies often use Subramaniam's compositions for stage presentations. In addition to writing scores for Hollywood movies such as *Little Buddha* and *Salaam Bombay*, Subramaniam has also contributed to ballets.

Subramaniam married Vijayashree, herself a talented classical musician. The couple travelled, toured and performed together on fusion projects. A few years after her death in 1995, he tied the knot with popular film playback singer Kavita Krishnamurthy. His brothers, L. Shankar and L. Vaidyanathan, are also acclaimed musicians. Subramaniam's children are also talented performing artistes.

In collaboration with his late wife, Subramaniam wrote a book on music, titled *Euphony*. He has also put together a set of four CDs titled *An Anthology of South Indian Music*, to explain the concepts of the classical music of south India.

In 1992, he initiated the Lakshminarayana Global Music Festival, one of the world's most reputed travelling music festivals conducted on a grand scale, bringing together legends from all over the world to perform on one stage. The festival has been held in over twenty countries so far.

In recognition to his priceless contribution to the world of music, Subramaniam has been awarded the Padma Bhushan and the Padma Shri. He was honoured as Nada Chakravarti (literally 'emperor of sound'). He was also honoured as 'The Most Creative Artist' by the prestigious Sangeet Natak Akademi. In 1981, this musical legend earned a nomination for the prestigious Grammy Award. The Universities of Madras and Bangalore have also conferred honorary doctorates on him.

Subramaniam has established his unique identity through his universal approach and gracefully redefined the possibility of instrumental fusion at the international level. The world is waiting for more masterpieces from this great violinist who has successfully crossed frontiers to take musical compositions into the global arena.

The Spirit of Conquest

Name: Lakshmi Niwas Mittal
Birth Date: 15 June 1950
Place: Sadulpur, Rajasthan

In 1976, this astute businessman made a move that was the first of several path-breaking steps. He acquired a run-down loss-making steel mill in Indonesia. It was the first of many such acquisitions he was to make, as he continued buying out unprofitable steel plants and turning them around into viable ventures. This novel strategy saw the meteoric rise of Ispat International, the company that Lakshmi Mittal founded.

Following Ispat International's merger with LMN Holdings in 2004, it came to be known as Mittal Steel. The company's growth spurt continued and, in 2006, Mittal Steel merged with Europe's largest steel producer, Arcelor, to become ArcelorMittal. It is currently the globe's largest steel company, and Mittal is among the world's wealthiest people. Steel from ArcelorMittal, which today has a presence in twenty countries across four continents, helps build many of our cars, household appliances and buildings among other things. The company's core philosophy is to produce 'safe, sustainable steel'.

Mittal's climb to the top reflects tremendous focus, determination, foresight and risk taking ability, and that's what makes his story more than ordinary.

Mittal spent the first five years of his life in Sadulpur, a remote village in Rajasthan, where even the concept of running water seemed far-fetched. However, his family soon moved to Calcutta, where his father set up a small steel mill. Mittal obtained his degree in commerce from St Xavier's College. He also had his first experience of running a business at his father's venture. In 1976, when he went to Indonesia on work, he spotted an opportunity in the Indonesian steel plant and convinced his father to back him in buying it. The rest, as they say, is history.

Mittal knew that even though demand for steel was on the decline in the US and Europe at the time, the industry in Asia was in growth mode. He also envisioned that steel companies could become profitable if they grew enough to negotiate on an even keel with suppliers and customers. Such foresight helped him stay focused on expanding his business enterprises.

Mittal is appreciated for the role he has played in restructuring and consolidating the global steel industry. He is also regarded as a pioneer in the use of direct reduced iron as a substitute for scrap in the steel-making process. He currently serves as the director of Goldman Sachs, which deals in investment banking and financial services.

Mittal was named Business Person of 2006 by *Sunday Times*, International Newsmaker of the Year 2006 by *Time* and Person of the Year 2006 by *Financial Times*. In 2007, he was presented with a fellowship from King's College, London. He also received the 2007 Dwight D. Eisenhower Global Leadership Award and the Grand Cross of Civil Merit from Spain. In 2008, he was awarded the Padma Vibhushan and also chosen for the Forbes Lifetime Achievement Award.

Mittal's ambitious nature has always been backed by his perseverance, never-say-die attitude and diverse interests. His home in Kensington Palace Gardens, London, known as 'Taj Mittal', is decorated with stone from the same quarry that provided material for the Taj Mahal. He co-owns Queens Park Rangers Football Club. He has set up the Mittal's Champions Trust to support Indian athletes who have world-class potential. He has established a management institute in New Delhi.

Today, Mittal is an inspiration to many youngsters in India. He stands testimony to the fact that anyone with drive and vision can make it big in the world.

Melody Queen

Name: Lata Mangeshkar
Birth Date: 28 September 1929
Place: Indore, Madhya Pradesh

Meri awaaz hee pehchaan hai, sings Lata Mangeshkar in the 1977 film, *Kinara.* Indeed her voice is her identity. She is undoubtedly one of the most gifted playback singers of our country, and she has reigned over the Indian music industry for over sixty years. The 'Melody Queen' has garnered millions of fans all over the world with her rare sense of rhythm and charming voice. In her fulfilling professional journey, she has delivered several evergreen songs and successful stage performances. She not only captured the attention of audiences in her prime years but also continues to impress the current generation with her engaging renditions.

Lata hails from a family of art lovers. Her father Pandit Deenanath Mangeshkar owned a theatrical company. She received little formal education but was trained rigorously in music from her childhood. When her father died during her early teens, the responsibility of running the family fell on her shoulders. She started her professional journey when she was just thirteen years old. After a brief stint in the movies, she chose to pursue a career in the world of music.

Her first Hindi song '*Paa lagoon kar jori*' was released in 1946 but was not immediately popular. The following year, a producer rejected her thin, high-pitched voice. She eventually hit the right chords with other music directors in the industry. Her tremendously enriched voice surprised her initial critics. Her work went on to be appreciated in movies like *Mughal-e-Azam*, *Guide*, *Pakeezah*, *Abhimaan*, *Kora Kaagaz*, and *Lekin*, to name just a few.

Lata is well versed in many music genres like bhajans, classical music, ghazals and pop in addition to film songs. She has sung in more than thirty languages and rendered about 30,000 solos apart from contributing to famous duets and chorus-backed songs. She was also listed in the *Guinness Books of World Records* for some time as the most widely recorded artist in history.

Lata has had a long association with many directors and producers and enjoyed a clout that even leading movie stars could not once dream of. She has seen numerous transformations in the music industry and come a long way, adding feathers to her many caps. Her phenomenal hard work and discipline took her to the pinnacle of stardom as she delivered unforgettable blockbuster hits in tinseltown by singing in over 1,000 Hindi movies.

Lata's voice has such beautiful nuances and emotions that music lovers are enraptured. *Aye mere watan ke logon, zara ankh mein bhar lo pani,* her famous song released during the India–China war in 1962, is said to have moved then Prime Minister Jawaharlal Nehru to tears.

After winning numerous awards and recognitions, including the Bharat Ratna, in 1969, she made the unusual gesture of giving up the Filmfare Award for best female playback singer to promote fresher talent.

Now in her eighties, Lata makes rare public appearances and sings occasionally to keep her musical journey alive. She has also composed and directed music for films. Lata was nominated as a member of the Rajya Sabha in 1999. She is also the first Indian to have performed at the Royal Albert Hall.

Lata's creativity extends to many other spheres. Inspired by her ancestral jewellery, she came up with the Swaranjali collection for Adora, a diamond export company, which was auctioned off for charity. In 1999, she launched Lata, Eau de Parfum, a fragrance that gained instant acceptance in the market.

An introvert by nature, Lata admires actor Amitabh Bachchan and loves to watch television in her free time. She is also fond of cricket and is active on social networking sites. Photography is another of her passions. Chekov and Tolstoy are her favourite writers.

The Tennis Ace

Name: Leander Adrian Paes
Birth Date: 17 June 1973
Place: Calcutta, West Bengal

This champion tennis player has scripted several stunning victories during his successful stint in solo, doubles and mixed doubles tournaments at the national and international levels. His most fruitful collaboration was with Mahesh Bhupathi; the duo, nicknamed 'Indian Express', won numerous titles representing India. His charm, authoritativeness and never-say-die attitude on and off the court has made him one of India's most respected sportspersons.

Leander was educated at La Martiniere for Boys in Kolkata and later went to college in Chennai. He received formal training in tennis at Britannia Amritraj Tennis Academy. Vece Paes, his father, had played in the Indian hockey team during the 1972 Munich Olympics. His mother Jennifer captained the Indian basketball team at the Asian Basketball Championship in 1980.

Paes shot to fame in 1990 when he won the

Wimbledon Junior title and clinched top ranking, establishing himself as a promising player. He has won the US Open Championship apart from thirteen international Grand Slam titles—in doubles and mixed doubles events. His most recent wins have been at the Australian Open and at Miami, both in 2012. He has represented India in five Olympic events and is one of the few tennis players to have won Wimbledon titles in three decades. His other notable success was winning a bronze at the Atlanta Olympic Games in 1996, for which he was awarded the Rajiv Gandhi Khel Ratna.

Paes and Bhupathi successfully partnered in top tennis tournaments. In 1998, they played in the semi-finals of three Grand Slam tournaments: US Open, French Open, and Australian Open. In 1999, they created a record by playing in the finals of all four Grand Slam tournaments—they won the Wimbledon and French Open and became the first Indian pair to win the doubles title at any Grand Slam. However, their relationship then began to decline and, after 2006, they have played very few tournaments together. Paes has also paired up with Sébastien Lareau and Jan Siemerink for men's doubles and with Lisa Raymond and Martina Navratilova for mixed doubles.

Paes carried the Indian flag during the opening ceremony at the 2000 Sydney Olympics. A few weeks after winning the Wimbledon mixed doubles in 2003 with Navratilova, he was suspected of having a brain tumour, which later turned out to be a parasitic infection. This was a major turning point in his life and he refrained from playing in the US Open during his recovery period.

Paes had begun writing his autobiography in 1999 to share his triumphs, his feelings of patriotism and his struggle with obstacles during his rise into the limelight. However, the trauma of his treatment changed his perspective towards life. Following his recovery, his career went into roller coaster mode, and he tasted a mixture of victory and defeat. At the Doha Asian Games in 2006, he captained the Indian tennis squad and won two golds, for the men's doubles (with Mahesh Bhupathi) and mixed doubles (with Sania Mirza).

This former captain of the Davis Cup team is a recipient of the prestigious Padma Shri and continues to impress younger players. He is also associated with the Olympic Gold Quest Foundation set up by Prakash Padukone and Geet Sethi to nurture aspiring sportsmen and train them for participation in the Olympic Games.

The Captain of Captains

Name: Mahendra Singh Dhoni
Birth Date: 7 July 1981
Place: Ranchi, now in Jharkhand

One of the coolest captains in the history of Indian cricket, Mahendra Singh Dhoni, nicknamed Mahi, has come a long way from being a village lad to perhaps India's most admired cricketer.

Born to Pan Singh and Devaki Devi, Mahi was the youngest sibling among three, the others being sister Jayanti and brother Narendra. As a child, Mahi was attracted towards badminton and football, not cricket. He was the goalkeeper for a local football team and was once sent to play cricket for a local cricket club by the coach. Though he had not played cricket before, he impressed everyone with his wicketkeeping skills and soon became the regular wicketkeeper at Commando Cricket Club, Ranchi.

Dhoni debuted in the Bihar state cricket team in the 1998-99 cricket season and was selected to represent India A on a tour to Kenya in 2004. He scored multiple centuries against the Pakistan A team in a tri-nation series and was selected for the Indian national team later in the same year. The young man was soon noticed for his sense of style along with his cricketing skills. His long hair became a fad but it is rumoured that Dhoni himself is a fan of actor John Abraham, and chopped off his locks when John did so.

Dhoni's One-Day international (ODI) debut came in December 2004 against Bangladesh. Unfortunately, he was run out on the first ball he faced. However, in his fifth ODI against Pakistan in Visakhapatnam, Dhoni came to the crease after the fall of the first wicket and scored 148 runs off just 123 balls. He hit fifteen boundaries and four sixes. That was when he earned his first Man of the Match award.

On 2 December 2005, Dhoni made his Test cricket debut against Sri Lanka in Chennai. On 7 August 2007, he was named captain of India's Twenty20 team for the World Cup. Under his captaincy, India won the 2007 ICC World Twenty20 championship. He also led India to the number one position in the ICC Test rankings for the first time in 2009. Under his leadership, India won the ICC World Cup in 2011, beating Sri Lanka.

He is now captain of India in all three forms of the game and also captained Chennai Super Kings to victory in the Indian Premier League 2011. He is respected for his team spirit and the confidence he instills in the boys. One finds him always poised and honest, supportive to his team and optimistic of the future.

Dhoni has also been the recipient of many awards including the ICC ODI Player of the Year Award in 2008 and 2009. He is the first Indian player to achieve this feat. He has also been honoured with the Rajiv Gandhi Khel Ratna and Padma Shri. In 2011, the Indian Army conferred on him the title of Lieutenant Colonel; he is the only cricketer apart from Kapil Dev to have received this honour.

Dhoni married Sakshi Rawat in July 2010 in Dehra Dun, in a quiet family affair. The couple together work for the Sakshi Rawat Foundation, which offers help to orphaned children.

Dhoni's hobbies include listening to music, especially *ghazals*. Lata Mangeshkar and Kishore Kumar are his favourite singers. He is also fond of riding fast bikes and playing computer games. Among his idols are Bollywood superstar Amitabh Bachchan and cricketers Sachin Tendulkar and Adam Gilchrist.

Dhoni currently endorses over twenty brands, from apparel to sports goods, from mobile phones to beverages. He continues to awe people with his performance as a player and team leader. He is surely an icon of our times.

The Mani Magic

Name: Mani Ratnam
Birth Date: 2 June 1956
Place: Madurai, Tamil Nadu

Gopala Ratnam Subramaniam was the son of an established south Indian producer popularly known as Venus Gopalratnam. Though film-making was in Gopala's genes, he started his career as a management consultant.

After a few years, he wanted to explore the world of making quality moviemaking, though he had no formal training or degree in film-making, leave alone any experience in directing. Despite all this, curiosity and raw zeal got the better of him and he went on to direct his first film *Pallavi Anu Pallavi* in 1983. It was not very successful commercially but did receive critical acclaim and went on to win the Karnataka State Award for best screenplay.

Following this, he directed three more movies in Malayalam and Tamil. While the music of his films became a huge hit, their box office performances were average. Gopala considered this phase as his apprentice period and continued experimenting.

His perseverance paid off soon. His next film transformed his career graph. A romantic drama with a realistic screenplay, *Mouna Ragam* was an instant hit. A favourite among urban south Indians since then, this film boosted the director's confidence and he has never ever looked back. Gopala, who revolutionized film-making, is popularly known to all of us as Mani Ratnam.

Shooting for film songs was never considered serious business until Mani started making movies. In fact, moviegoers used to take breaks when songs were played on screen! Mani put in special efforts to visit exotic locales in India and shoot his song sequences. While most Indian directors tend to travel abroad in search of locations, Mani discovered some indigenous unexplored locales that were enchanting and breathtaking.

After *Mouna Ragam*, Mani worked on some of his best works. *Nayagan*, inspired by *The Godfather*, ranks in *Time*'s list of All-Time 100 Greatest Movies.

Mani's movies are appreciated for the themes he chooses as well as for the brilliant plot treatment. While his films like *Geethanjali* and *Anjali* deal with intense emotions, *Thiruda Thiruda* and *Alaipaayudhe* are light-hearted comedies. *Roja* and *Bombay* tackle political unrest in a refreshing manner. Notably, most of the critical moments in his films are shot either in rain or on a train. The song *Chhaiyya Chhaiyya*, shot atop a moving train for the Shah Rukh Khan starrer *Dil Se*, is etched in our collective memory.

Mani's technicians and actors find it an invaluable experience to work with him. While many directors act out a scene to the performers, Mani just explains the scene and asks them to experience the emotions and come out with original expressions. This evokes the best in his actors and technicians, who get a chance to engage themselves proactively in the moviemaking process as they explore their individuality and creativity.

Pithy dialogues, magical silences, stunning camera work, well-written scripts, exotic cinematography, flawless editing, haunting music and good aesthetics are some of the most popular aspects of Mani's magical film-making.

Mani married award-winning actress Suhasini in 1988. The couple set up Madras Talkies. It became a popular banner for distribution and production of TV serials and movies. Despite delivering numerous blockbusters, the humble director, who is also a Padma Shri winner, still believes that every movie he shoots is a new experience for him and he still has a lot more to learn. In fact, he has gone on record to say: 'I don't know how to make a film!'

The Barefoot Artist

Name: Maqbool Fida Husain
Birth Date: 17 September 1915
Place: Pandharpur, Maharashtra
Death Date: 9 June 2011
Place: London, United Kingdom

A world-famous artist once walked into a swanky Bombay club for dinner with a friend. While his host may have revelled in the company of the great painter, this obviously had little influence on the steward. The latter refused to serve at the table and asked the host to request his guest to leave. The reason? The man was not wearing shoes!

The host, a long-standing member of the club, argued and attempted to convince the authorities but in vain. The matter went to court and the club's decision was upheld. The man who had been recognized and appreciated for his art all over the world was in the news because he wore no footwear.

He was one of India's most public artists, who often created his paintings standing barefoot amid large audiences. His habit of going everywhere and all the time without shoes became his signature style. In fact, he went barefoot even to the Parliament. Popular opinion on this was divided. While some accepted it as a personal choice, others thought it disrespectful, considering that he could obviously 'afford shoes'.

For such reasons and other unusual acts, this famous Indian painter always courted controversy. He was none other than Maqbool Fida Husain, popularly known as M.F. Husain. Did he shy away from the controversies he created? No. Husain had the courage of conviction. As for his shoelessness, he dismissed the allegations of disrespect and attributed it to health reasons.

Husain hailed from a traditional Muslim background. He lost his mother when he was an infant. Some time later, his father remarried and moved to Indore, where Maqbool did his schooling. As a child, he learnt the art of calligraphy and developed a passion for poetry. After having painted many countryside landscapes and completed his schooling, Husain moved to Bombay in 1935. There, he joined the J.J. School of Arts.

In the initial years, Husain earned his livelihood by painting billboards for movies. In 1947, he joined the Progressive Artists' Group founded by Francis Newton Souza. He won an award at the annual exhibition of Bombay Art Society, and this marked the beginning of a successful career. Husain went on to become the highest paid painter in India. His single canvases fetched up to two million dollars at recent auctions. He held his first solo exhibition in Zurich in 1952 and, over the following years, his work was showcased across Europe and the US. Husain was invited along with Pablo Picasso to the Sao Paulo Biennial. *Forbes* called him the 'Picasso of India'.

In 1955, Husain was awarded the prestigious Padma Shri by the Government of India. He then produced his first award-winning film, *Through the Eyes of a Painter,* shown at the Berlin Film Festival in 1967. Later, he produced *Gaja Gamini* and *Meenaxi: A Tale of Three Cities.* He was awarded the Padma Bhushan in 1973 and nominated to the Rajya Sabha in 1986. In 1991, he was presented with the Padma Vibhushan.

Husain's movies as well as his paintings depicting Hindu deities in socially unacceptable forms stirred controversies and he was charged with hurting popular sentiment. At the age of ninety-two, when he was nominated for the prestigious Raja Ravi Varma Award, cultural organizations protested and obtained an interim order to stay the granting of the award. Cases piled up in court against him, starting in 1996 after a Hindi periodical published an inflammatory article on his paintings done in the 1970s. Fanatical mobs harassed him and vandalized his exhibits. A genuine and committed artist, who worked in the spirit of modernity, progress and tolerance, was thus driven into exile. The Indian legal system failed to facilitate his safe return.

2006 onwards, Husain lived in Dubai and London. He travelled across the world except to India. In early

2010, he was conferred Qatar nationality, something that is very rare. He accepted this honour but also expressed deep regret that he would have to give up his Indian citizenship.

Even in his nineties, the artist worked long hours producing large paintings and sculptures. One could love him or hate him but never ignore him. Despite all the controversies, Husain was an icon among artists of the whole world. He did not belong to any particular country.

The Flying Sikh

Name: Milkha Singh
Birth Date: 8 October 1935
Place: Lyallpur, now Pakistan

He won seventy-seven of the eighty races that he participated in during his glorious years as an athlete. For over four decades, he reigned supreme as the only Indian to have broken an Olympic record. This genius sprinter proved his mettle at a time when there were neither sophisticated facilities available to practise nor alluring rewards for winners.

It was an uphill task to achieve this kind of success, after what he went through during the Partition in 1947. At the age of twelve, Milkha Singh saw his parents butchered before his eyes and had to escape to India amidst corpses on a train!

The iron-willed youth faced the world alone with little emotional support. Struggling against odds he dared to write his own destiny. He was rejected three times when he tried to join the army. It was then that he discovered his penchant for running and was determined to become the best sprinter of his era.

Rigorous practice sessions followed on the banks of the Yamuna and up the steep hills nearby to hone his craft. He even tried competing with a running train and, as a result, vomited blood, and collapsed in exhaustion. He kept pushing himself and conditioned his body to run two races in one day. The pursuit continued as he kept accumulating easy victories in his kitty.

After his successful stint at the Cuttack National Games, Asian Games, as well as the Commonwealth Games in the late 1950s, the Helms Trophy winner missed the bronze in the 1960 Rome Olympics in a photo finish. He was so dejected by this defeat that he almost hung up his running shoes until he was called back later to compete with another leading athlete in Pakistan named Abdul Khaliq. He easily won this contest and was given the name 'The Flying Sikh' by Ayub Khan, the former President of Pakistan.

A few years later, Milkha donated all his sporting treasures including his running shoes, uniforms, blazers, medals, souvenirs and trophies to the nation. Recently he gave away his Olympic running shoes to be auctioned for charity for the benefit of the blind and of needy children. He has also adopted the son of a Kargil matyr and taken up the responsibility of his upbringing.

A perfect disciplinarian, Milkha follows a regular fitness routine that includes jogging, golfing and gymming. He is the proud father of Jeev Milkha Singh, an acclaimed Indian golfer, and encourages his son to restore the glory that he had lost at Rome decades ago.

Milkha's inspirational story is part of several school textbooks, and his achievements linger on in the minds and hearts of millions of Indians.

Being honoured with the Padma Shri and the Arjuna Award was more than just recognition for this extraordinary athlete who started off at a wage of ten rupees and went on to become a legend. He has set up an athletic academy in Chandigarh to train budding athletes. *Bhaag Milkha Bhaag*, a biographical sports drama based on Milkha Singh's life, is under production.

Mystic Woman

Name: Mirabai
Birth Date: AD 1498
Place: Merta, Rajasthan
Death Date: AD 1547
Place: Rajasthan

Ratan Singh Rathor, a Rajput chieftain, was once gifted a beautiful idol of Lord Krishna by an ascetic. His three-year-old daughter was captivated by its beauty. She resolved that Krishna would be her friend throughout her life. Despite the criticism and challenges she faced all her life due to this resolution, she never wavered from her commitment and proved her devotion for her beloved Giridhar till her last breath.

This little girl was none other than Mirabai, the granddaughter of the founder of Jodhpur. Even as a very young child, Mira showed religious tendencies and her mother was quite supportive of her interests. One day, when the little Mira saw a wedding procession passing by her mansion, she innocently asked her mother who her husband would be. Her mother replied, partly in jest and partly serious, 'Why, you already have your husband. . . Shri Krishna!' This stuck on in Mirabai's mind and heart all her life.

In 1516, Mira's father arranged her wedding with Prince Bhoj Raj, the son of Rana Sanga of Chittor, the scion of a wealthy and influential family. The splendour and luxury did not affect Mira who just went about her duties by day and spent all her evenings singing praises of her beloved Krishna whom she called 'the saviour of mankind'.

Here is an extract from one of her songs:

That dark dweller in Braj
Is my only refuge.
O my companion,
Worldly comfort is an illusion,
As soon as you get it, it goes.
I have chosen the indestructible for my refuge.
Him whom the snake of death
Will not devour.
My beloved dwells in my heart.
I have actually seen that Abode of Joy.
Mira's Lord is Giridhari, the Indestructible.
My Lord, I have taken refuge with thee,
Thy slave.

However, this unconditional devotion to her lord and her spiritual discussions with various sages did not go down too well with her husband's family. Besides, Mira refused to worship Goddess Durga, the family deity. This made their disappointment more intense. Added to this, Mira's sister-in-law Udabai spread baseless gossip about Mirabai entertaining men in her chamber. Provoked by these stories, her husband barged into her room one day, sword in hand, only to find Mirabai alone, and ecstatic, singing paeans to her beloved Giridhar.

There are interesting legends of how Krishna rescued her from her detractors. One such story says that as Mirabai's fame gradually spread far and wide, the Mughal emperor Akbar wanted to meet the princess who was a living saint. Since Akbar was an enemy of Rana Sanga, he disguised himself and visited the temple where Mira sang her *bhajans*. He was so carried away by her music that he gifted her a necklace. When Bhoj Raj found out, he ordered Mirabai to drown herself in the river. It is said that Krishna appeared before her and asked her to go to Vrindavan. Mirabai dutifully left the palace along with some followers. When Bhoj Raj realized his folly, he requested her to return and she did.

According to another tale, her in-laws once sent her a cobra in a basket on the pretext of a message. When it reached her, it turned into an idol of Krishna with a garland of flowers. They even tried to poison her but the poison turned to nectar when Mira offered it to her beloved Giridhar before partaking of it herself.

When Bhoj Raj lost his life fighting the Mughals, Mirabai was asked to commit *sati* but she refused, boldly stating that she considered Krishna as her real husband. One of her poems corroborates this: '*Sati na hosyan girdhar gansyan mhara man moho ghananami*' ['I will not commit sati. I will sing the songs of Giridhari, as He is my real husband.'] Soon after, she left the palace for good, went to Vrindavan and became a disciple of Guru Ravidas.

At Vrindavan, she wanted to engage in theological discussion with Rup Goswami, the celibate disciple of Chaitanya Mahaprabhu. Goswami refused on the grounds that he didn't talk to women. Mirabai replied: 'There is only one true man in Vrindavan (universe) and that is Krishna. All the rest are *gopis* to Krishna.' On hearing this, Rup Goswami realized the wisdom of Mirabai and agreed to the discourse.

Mirabai spent the rest of her life in Vrindavan. Shortly before her death, she moved to Dwarka.

Indians look upon her as an incarnation of Radha, the sweetheart of Krishna. She was an embodiment of love and innocence. Mirabai composed 200 poems that were simple and unpretentious, yet expressed her intense spiritual fervour.

As Swami Sivananda, a proponent of Vedanta and yoga puts it: 'Mira's songs infuse faith, courage, devotion and love of God in the minds of the readers. They inspire the aspirants to take to the path of devotion and produce in them a marvellous thrill and a melting of the heart.'

The Philosopher Poet

Name: Mirza Asadullah Beg Khan
Birth Date: 27 December 1797
Place: Agra, Uttar Pradesh
Death Date: 15 February 1869
Place: Delhi

He is said to have remarked once that although his poetry didn't receive its due during his lifetime, people would not fail to realize its greatness after his death. How true his words have turned out to be! Even today, more than a century after his death, he is hailed as one of the greatest Urdu poets ever.

Mirza Ghalib was born in Agra into an aristocratic family of Turkish descent. His birth name was Mirza Asadullah Beg Khan. After he became a poet, he chose the pseudonym 'Ghalib', meaning 'the superior one' or 'the all-conquering one'.

Ghalib's father died when was about five years old. His uncle took on the responsibility of raising Ghalib and his two brothers, but he too passed away three years later. Ghalib was then left under the care of his mother's family. He had an arranged marriage at thirteen with Umrao Begum, and moved to Delhi thereafter. Many scholars detect the influence of these events of his life on his poetry.

Ghalib never really had a steady income, though he was associated for a while with the court of the Mughal emperor Bahadur Shah Zafar II. He survived mostly on the generosity of his friends and patrons. He had a love for the good things in life but never had enough money to fulfil all his desires. His great wit and conversation skills, however, are legendary.

Interestingly, Ghalib lived in the period that saw the decline of the Mughal Empire and the expanding power of the British. Many events of this period are chronicled in his poetry. The declining Mughal nobility was something that he was part of, so he was able to provide a first-hand account of the turbulence of the times.

Ghalib's poetry also dealt with themes like love, man's place and purpose in the universe, human nature and the nature of life itself. His writings were often philosophical, reflecting a deep understanding of several subjects. Apart from Urdu, he also wrote in Persian. His best poetic works were written before he turned twenty-one. Here is an instance of Ghalib's poetry (with translation):

Rahiye ab aisi jagah chal kar jahaan koi na ho
Humsukhan koi na ho aur humzabaan koi na ho

Baydaron deewar sa ik ghar banana chahiye
Koi humsaya na ho aur pasbaan koi na ho

Padhariye ghar beemar to koi na ho timardar
Aur agar mar jaayein to nohakhwaan koi na ho

(I wish to go and dwell,
In such a place,
Where there's no one else.
No one to understand my speech,
No one around to talk with,
There, I want to reach.

I wish to build,
One such house,
Without a door to enter
Without the boundary walls,
Thus there will be no neighbours,
And there will be no guard.

There will be no one thus,
To take care of me,
When I will fall ill.
And there will be no one,
To mourn or cry.)

Apart from his poetry, his innumerable letters to his
friends and admirers have also held people enthralled,
due to their uniquely conversational, light-hearted

and engaging style. He is believed to have written four to five letters every day and his Urdu prose is as remarkable as his poetry.

Ghalib was sceptical of institutionalized religion but emphasized a personal relationship with god. He was also irreverent about many social norms and structures and led life on his own terms. Refusing to give up his hedonistic ways right to the end, he died in penury at the age of seventy-two, plagued by alcoholism and health problems. He was left with no survivors, as none of his seven children survived infancy.

His life and works have been depicted through films and serials, not only in India but also in Pakistan and his ghazals have been rendered by many renowned singers.

In 1969, a hundred years after Ghalib's death, the Ghalib Academy was established in New Delhi. It is intended to be a literary and cultural landmark that immortalizes the life and works of Ghalib. Recently, Ghalib's house in Chandni Chowk was renovated and made into a museum showcasing his belongings and his works.

Voice of Versatility

Name: Mohammed Rafi
Birth Date: 24 December 1924
Place: Punjab, British India
Death Date: 31 July 1980
Place: Bombay, Maharashtra

A long time ago, the composer duo Laxmikant–Pyarelal wanted Mohammed Rafi to sing a few songs for their debut film. However, they were not in a position to pay the remuneration Rafi commanded. When Rafi heard of their dilemma, he told them that they should just go ahead and make arrangements for the recording; matters of money could be thought about later. Laxmikant–Pyarelal did as told and the recordings were soon completed. They offered a fee to Rafi but he returned it graciously as a token of his good wishes for their debut.

There are many such anecdotes about Rafi's magnanimity. In another instance, he helped a struggling composer by lending his stupendous voice for as little as a rupee!

Born in a village near Amritsar, Rafi grew up in Lahore, where a member of his family noticed his talent and encouraged him to learn classical music. He then started performing at concerts and also for All India Radio's Lahore station. He moved to Bombay at the age of twenty, took up a small room and performed his riyaz diligently.

He gradually rose from his humble beginnings to reach the highest echelons of Bollywood playback singing. This was largely due to his amazing versatility as a singer. He could endow his songs with myriad emotions based on the characterization and situation being depicted—longing, mischief, sorrow, romance, and everything in between. He was the leading male Bollywood playback singer during the 1950s and 1960s. While he sang for all the leading heroes of the time, including Guru Dutt, Dev Anand and Shammi Kapoor, he had himself attained heroic status and a vast fan following.

It is remarkable how Rafi's rendition of songs always perfectly matched the mannerisms of the actor on whom the song was filmed. Shammi Kapoor, for whom Rafi sang in many successful movies, remarked that Rafi always seemed to know how the hero would perform on screen and sang accordingly.

Rafi had an extremely successful working partnership with renowned composers like Naushad, Madan Mohan, Shankar Jaikishen, O.P. Nayyar, and S.D. Burman. Rafi sang many duets with Lata Mangeshkar and Asha Bhonsle. *Pyaasa, Chaudhvin Ka Chand, Naya Daur, Kashmir Ki Kali,* and *Dil Apna Aur Preet Parai* are some films he sang for. He won numerous Filmfare Awards and National Film Awards. He was also honoured with the Padma Shri.

Rafi's popularity was eclipsed when actor–singer Kishore Kumar began to make a name for himself as a playback singer. Rafi receded into the background for about five years but made a comeback in the 1970s, singing qawaalis for actors like Rishi Kapoor in movies like *Amar Akbar Anthony*. Rafi also went on to win national awards for songs like *Kya hua tera wada* recorded for the film *Hum Kisi Se Kum Nahin*

Although he died of heart failure in 1980, his legacy lives on. People continue to visit his burial site in Mumbai. Many musical concerts are dedicated to him. Several singers over the years have tried to imitate his style of singing and some have found admirers by virtue of the fact that they sound like Rafi.

Bapu, Father of the Nation

Name: Mohandas Karamchand Gandhi
Birth Date: 2 October 1869
Place: Porbundar, British India
Death Date: 30 January 1948
Place: New Delhi

We, the citizens of India, have enjoyed more than half a century of independence, thanks to the efforts of the courageous patriots who claimed *swaraj* ('self-rule') for India from the British through their relentless freedom struggle.

Many parts of the world fought for independence with war and weapons but the approach of the Indian subcontinent was quite different, thanks to the path-breaking initiatives and staunch ideals of this spiritual leader. Mohandas Karamchand Gandhi strove, unflinchingly and uncompromisingly, for liberty through truth and ahimsa ('non-violence').

Gandhiji believed in social protest and 'passive resistance'. This new approach was termed by his nephew as *sadagraha* and later modified by Gandhi himself to *satyagraha*, meaning 'soul-force' or 'truth-force'.

He discovered his spirituality during his teenage years when he got an opportunity to travel to England for higher studies. In those days, foreign travel was considered taboo, or almost a sin. Moreover, Gandhi had been married Kasturba when he was barely thirteen years old. In order to travel abroad he now had to leave her behind along with his child, who was then a few months old. However, he did not want to lose this golden opportunity.

Gandhi studied law in London and returned to India in 1891. He worked briefly in Bombay and Rajkot and then left for South Africa, where he lived for over two decades and where he faced first-hand the realities of racial discrimination. His experiences in this country shaped his political views and laid the foundation of his social activism.

Once he returned to India in 1915, Gandhiji joined the Indian National Congress and soon rose to a position of leadership. He set about not only to demand home rule for India but also to bring about reformation within its society. He was imprisoned several times on account of sedition but carried on with his efforts at achieving independence for India. He led several campaigns to fight poverty, gender discrimination and untouchability. He renamed the untouchables as Harijans or 'children of God', set up a common kitchen at the Satyagraha Ashram at Sabarmati, Gujarat, and accepted a Harijan family within the premises. He faced staunch opposition for this act and the flow of funds to run the ashram suddenly ceased. However, Gandhiji stood by his decision, confident that the Almighty would recognize his good intentions and send help. His belief proved true when a wealthy merchant suddenly arrived from nowhere and donated a lot of money to the ashram!

Gandhiji's shaven head, traditional Indian dhoti as well as the shawl made of self-spun cloth marked his simplicity. Winston Churchill, the British prime minister, referred to him as a 'half-naked fakir'. The name Mahatma meaning 'the great soul' was given to him by Rabindranath Tagore. He was known all over the world for his famous speeches. He believed that if one has faith in God, he need not fear anybody else. He transformed the thinking of the masses through the power of his words and preached equal rights for all. When the Meenakshi Temple in Madurai barred entry of Harijans, he refused to enter the temple until the restriction was lifted. He also raised the slogan for 'Quit India' against the British. Later he staunchly opposed the partition of the nation.

On 30 January 1948, Gandhiji was shot while walking towards a prayer meeting. The entire nation mourned this assassination.

Decades after his death, Bapu, the Father of the Nation, remains immortal and is one of the most prominent personalities who comes to mind when we talk of our struggle for independence. His avatar is eternal in history.

Engineer, Statesman and Visionary

Name: Mokshagundam Vishweshwaraiah
Birth Date: 15 September 1860
Place: Muddenahalli, Mysore, Karnataka
Death Date: 14 April 1962
Place: Bangalore, Karnataka

A person who wanted to meet Sir Mokshagundam Vishweshwaraiah once made an appointment but was unable to reach on the given day and time. He turned up the next day though, without notice. Sir M. Vishweshwaraiah is said to have told the person, 'You have committed a double mistake—first, by not keeping the engagement yesterday, and second, by coming when you were not expected to.'

Many such anecdotes abound regarding Sir M. Vishweshwaraiah or Sir MV, as he came to be called. People who knew him recall him as being a staunch disciplinarian, a stickler for punctuality, and a man of honesty and integrity. Moreover, he was always immaculately dressed.

When a relative of his thanked him for some

financial help, Sir MV is said to have written to him saying, 'The best return you can show for any help you have received from me in the past is by maintaining integrity, efficiency, and generous disposition and a high character in every respect. I mention this to remind you that with age and circumstances, people are liable to change.'

Such was Sir MV's personality. His many admirable qualities made him stand out from the crowd from a very young age. He completed his high school and graduation in Bangalore. Always an excellent student, he received a scholarship to pursue civil engineering at the government college in Pune, after which he began his long and illustrious career at the Public Works Department in the erstwhile Bombay Presidency.

Sir MV built a reputation for himself as an engineer par excellence. He was instrumental in the construction of many large dams and water supply schemes, such as Tigra Dam in Gwalior and Krishna Raja Sagara Dam in Mysore. He was the brain behind automatic sluice gates, which are used in many dams today. All his life, he was passionate about appropriate utilization of water resources in India.

Sir MV later became the Chief engineer and then dewan (prime minister) of the erstwhile princely state of Mysore. People knew him not just as an engineer but also as a visionary. He had an aptitude and inclination for development in a number of fields apart from engineering.

Apart from irrigation, Sir MV also worked to improve drainage systems and construct roads. He was instrumental in the creation of Mysore University, University Vishweshwaraiah College of Engineering in Bangalore, University of Agricultural Sciences in Bangalore, Mysore Iron and Steel Works in Bhadravathi and State Bank of Mysore, among other establishments. Sir MV was a staunch supporter of industrialization, and his famed slogan was 'industrialize or perish'.

Sir MV was honoured as the Knight Commander of the Order of the Indian Empire in 1915. He received the Bharat Ratna in 1955.

It is said that Sir MV never used his various positions of power and influence to reap benefits for himself or others. When he was offered the position of dewan of Mysore, he told his relatives that he would accept the post on one condition alone—that they would promise not to ask him to use his official clout to bestow personal favours on them.

Sir MV stuck to his ideals till the time of his death at the ripe old age of 101. The several constructions he was involved in and the various institutions he built continue to benefit a large number of people across the country to this day. His birthday, 15 September, is celebrated as Engineers' Day in India.

Bhakta Meera

Name: M.S. Subbulakshmi
Birth Date: 16 September 1916
Place: Madurai, Tamil Nadu
Death Date: 11 December 2004
Place: Chennai, Tamil Nadu

In Madurai, every year during Ramnavami, festivals are organized and idols of Lord Rama are taken around town in an embellished chariot. Little Kunjamma often occupied a special place next to the deity on these rounds. Daughter of Shanmukhavadivu, a reputed veena player, and granddaughter of violinist Akkammal, she had an enviable musical lineage and could grasp the nuances of different ragas at a very young age. She constantly hummed along with the veena.

Kunjamma received formal training in Carnatic music under Srinivasa Iyengar, a well known singer of those times. Unfortunately, her guru passed away soon after her lessons began. Since Kunjamma suffered from whooping cough, she stopped formal schooling and became immersed in her own world of music with her favourite thambura. She also learnt how to play the mridangam and this enhanced her sense of rhythm.

Kunjamma fantasized about recording her songs—she held a rolled paper, a make-believe microphone, as she sang. Her dreams were realized when she recorded her first disc at the age of ten.

At a time when a Carnatic concert was a domain largely reserved for men, Kunjamma stunned her audience during a recital at the prestigious Madras Music Academy with her brilliant rendition of some famous bhajans. Veterans were astonished at how she could sing complicated musical notes with ease. This child and teen prodigy went on to become one of the most popular and successful Carnatic vocalists of all times.

Madurai Shanmukhavadivu Subbulakshmi, popular as M.S. Subbulakshmi or simply MS, was the first musician to receive the prestigious Bharat Ratna. MS broke all linguistic barriers and attracted fans equally from India and abroad when she delivered devotional songs flawlessly in more than ten languages including Tamil, Hindi, Sanskrit, Kannada, Telugu, and Malayalam.

In 1936, MS met her future husband, Sadasivam, a dynamic freedom fighter with a 'nothing is impossible' attitude. Sadasivam was already a father of two daughters, Radha and Vijaya, from his first marriage. After the death of his first wife, Sadasivam wed MS on 10 July 1940. The couple decided not to have more children. The doting husband offered unconditional support by involving himself in her career and boosting her image through the famous Tamil magazine *Kalki*, which he had co-founded.

MS also enjoyed a brief stint as an actress. Her debut film was *Sevasadanam* and she went on to play the lead role in the famous film *Bhakta Meera*. Her bhajans in this movie were instant hits; in fact, people love to listen to them even today. However, she soon stepped away from acting and chose to concentrate on music.

MS even has a colour named after her. Kancheepuram Muthu Chettiar was a famous saree merchant of those times. An ardent fan of MS, the master weaver gifted her a Kancheepuram silk saree in a unique blue shade with shots of black and green highlights. The saree was specially woven for her under his personal supervision and its distinctive blue shade became so famous at that time that it was named MS Blue!

MS and Sadasivam once decided that the money from all her musical concerts would be used for charitable purposes. She performed in over 200 charity concerts and donated lakhs of rupees to charity. The couple once again proved their integrity and earned tremendous respect when, during a financial low, they sold their posh house and moved to a much smaller rented accommodation to keep up their commitment. When her husband passed away in 1997, MS gave up public performances.

Some of her popular songs include *Suprabhatam, Vishnu sahasranamam, Hanuman Chalisa,*

Bhajagovindam, Vaishnava Janato, Hari Tuma Haro, and *Kurai Onrum Illai.* Any ardent fan of Carnatic music is sure to have the priceless musical collections of MS. *Sri Venkatesa Suprabhatam,* an album recorded in 1963, is still constantly in demand. In fact, the cover design has remained unchanged for decades.

A doctorate holder from several universities and a recipient of many prestigious awards like Padma Bhushan, Padma Vibhushan, Ramon Magsaysay Award and Sangeet Natak Akademi Award, MS passed away at the age of eighty-eight, leaving behind a rich and lasting musical legacy.

Father of the Green Revolution

Name: M.S. Swaminathan
Birth Date: 7 August 1925
Place: Kumbakonam, Tamil Nadu

Carpets of maize, rice, millet and wheat cover many parts of India. The country enjoys the labour of farmers who sweat in the fields to produce the necessary yields. However, if the seeds that they had planted beneath the soil were still the same as the ones our ancestors used, we would long ago have become slaves to famine or have had to import staple food.

Thanks to the sophisticated invention of this extraordinary agriculturist, India has not only become self-sufficient in the production of staple foods but has also become the leading exporter of grains to other countries, thus earning large revenues from overseas.

This brilliant genetic transformation in the field of agriculture was brought about by what is called 'The Green Revolution' and the pioneer and godfather of this exciting journey was none other than the Indian geneticist, Maankombu Sambasivan Swaminathan.

A few decades ago, India could not cater to the increasing food demands of its soaring population. Many other developing countries also lagged behind in food production. Famine was quite common in those times, claiming the lives of millions who died due to starvation.

Swaminathan, as a young boy, was highly influenced by the Gandhian principle of self-reliance and was against importing goods from other countries. He chose to study agriculture in college, as he wanted to make a tangible difference in this field. He did his post graduation from the Indian Agricultural Research Institute and went abroad for further studies in genetics, completing his doctorate from Cambridge University. He turned down the offer of lectureship abroad and returned to India at a time when staple foods were being imported, despite the fact that over 75 per cent of the population was employed in agriculture.

Swaminathan realized the potential danger and invested all his expertise in trying to improve quality and yield in the agricultural sector. He experimented with cross-breeding traditionally, using wheat grains with seeds from Mexico, and came up with hybrid wheat varieties that yielded much more grain. Further research was carried out on the same lines for rice, potato and jute. There was a ray of hope, hope of creating a socio-economic miracle.

However, this 'green' journey was not without challenges. When hybrid plants yielded more seeds, the crops initially collapsed due to the excess weight. Further research was needed to develop varieties with stronger stalks.

Swaminathan had to set up nearly 2,000 model farms to convince farmers to use the new varieties of seeds and increase yields. He also approached the government to import 18,000 tonnes of the new seed varieties. The government had many misgivings as famine was already prevalent at the time. However, there was no better way out than to take the risk and this earned him the required approval.

Only Punjab had the right infrastructure to reap the benefits of this new invention. Farmers all over India needed new pesticides and fertilizers but the food distribution networks were quite inefficient. Swaminathan received ample support from then Prime Minister Indira Gandhi, who gave him a free hand in leading the agricultural revolution. Such support helped him, to bring about the growth and development of sustainable agricultural practices in India.

A recipient of the prestigious World Food Prize, Swaminathan believes that farmers should adopt eco-friendly farming methods and insists that the potential of increasing the yields is not yet thoroughly exploited, that there is still a long way to go.

Considered the father of economic ecology, Swaminathan has started the M.S. Swaminathan Research Foundation that aims to eliminate hunger and poverty at the global level. It spreads awareness among farmers to adopt latest agricultural practices and adapt to the rapidly changing economy. Not surprisingly, he was ranked among the twenty most influential Asians of the twentieth century by *Time* magazine.

Swami Vivekananda

Name: Narendranath Dutta
Birth Date: 12 January 1863
Place: Calcutta, West Bengal
Death Date: 4 July 1902
Place: Calcutta, West Bengal

'Sisters and Brothers of America, it fills my heart with joy unspeakable to rise in response to the warm and cordial welcome which you have given us. I thank you in the name of the most ancient order of monks in the world; I thank you in the name of the mother of religions; and I thank you in the name of millions and millions of Hindu people of all classes and sects.'

These words were the beginning of his first brief address in the World Parliament of Religions, which opened on 11 September 1893 in Chicago. This eloquent speaker needs no introduction. He was Swami Vivekananda.

This disciple of Ramakrishna Paramhamsa and a world spokesperson for Vedanta received the name Swami Vivekananda only when he became a monk. He was born Narendranath (nicknamed Naren) to

Bhuvaneshwari Devi and Vishwanath Dutta in a traditional family in Kolkata. The story goes that his pious mother had prayed to Vireshwar Shiva of Varanasi to give her a son. Lord Shiva appeared in her dream and pledged that he would be born as her son.

As a child, Naren was vivacious and bold. Once, he and his friends were playing noisily in a garden. The owner of the garden threatened them, 'There is a demon on the tree who swallows up naughty children.' The other kids were frightened and took to their heels but Naren climbed the tree and settled down on a branch for several hours. The demon, of course, did not appear. Naren got down and declared the threat to be a hoax.

He was naughty but he was also a natural leader with tremendous power of self-control since his early childhood. His thinking and personality were influenced by both his parents. He inherited the rational, logical mind of his father and the religious temperament of his mother. No wonder he grew up to embrace the agnostic philosophies of the West and to worship science while, at the same time, nurturing a vehement desire to know the Truth and to realize God. Even as a child, he was adept at meditation and could enter a state of samadhi. His great fascination for wandering monks and his spirit of renunciation led him to give away things to beggars to the extent that once, on his birthday, he gave away his new clothes to a beggar who asked him for alms.

Naren had an amazing memory. He always performed

well in school and college. His power of concentration and alertness made Professor William Hastie, principal of Scottish Church College, where he was studying, comment, 'Narendra is really a genius. I have travelled far and wide but I have never come across a lad of his talents and possibilities.'

Once, in literature class, Hastie was explaining what 'trance' meant in William Wordsworth's poem, *The Excursion*. He mentioned that if anyone wanted to know the real meaning of the word, they should go to meet Ramakrishna of Dakshineswar, the only individual whom he had ever seen in this state. Naren decided to visit the saint.

Naren's meeting with Ramakrishna became the turning point in his life. Initially, he wondered how a spiritual guru who used such simple language could be a great teacher.

Naren asked, 'Do you believe in god, sir?'

The Paramhamsa replied, 'Yes.'

'Can you prove it?'

'Yes.'

'How?'

'Because I see Him just as I see you here, only in a much more intense sense.'

On one hand, Naren was thoroughly impressed by Ramakrishna but, on the other hand, he was not yet ready to accept him or his theory of Advaita and his obsession to be guided by the will of Goddess Kali. The Paramhamsa perplexed him. Naren visited him regularly. Ramakrishna never asked Naren to abandon reason and replied to his queries with: 'Try to see the truth from all angles.'

After Naren's father died, his family was hit by poverty and misery. Naren went to Ramakrishna and requested him to pray to Goddess Kali to help them out. Ramakrishna advised Naren to approach the goddess himself. Naren stood before the idol of Kali and entered a deep meditative state. To his dismay, he could not speak about his poverty. He repeatedly begged the Goddess: 'O Mother, bestow on me the spirit of renunciation. Let me see you, that is all I beg of you.'

After this incident, Naren wholeheartedly accepted Ramakrishna as his guru and surrendered completely to him. During his final days, Ramakrishna asked Naren to take care of the other disciples. After Ramakrishna passed away, all the disciples went to live in a rented place in Baranagar on the banks of the Ganga. This became the first math (monastery) of the disciples who constituted the Ramakrishna Order.

For the next five years, Naren travelled the length and breadth of India and acquainted himself with the diverse religious traditions and the different patterns of social life. He reached Kanyakumari on foot during Christmas Eve of 1892. There, he meditated on the rock, which later came to be known as Vivekananda Rock Memorial. It was in Madras that Naren came to be known as Swami Vivekananda.

Vivekananda then travelled to America. His address

at the Conference of World Religions in Chicago was highly applauded. He stressed the fact that no religion is superior and none is inferior. His speech made him a celebrity overnight. He was invited to many institutions all over the world. Wherever he went, he described the greatness of Indian culture and epitomized Hinduism. In London, Margaret Nobel, later named 'Nivedita', became one of his many disciples. She came to India and settled here. After four years of travelling in the West, Vivekananda returned to India.

Vivekananda believed that the Vedanta philosophy was the essence of Hinduism. He preached that the greatest religion is to be true to your own nature. He taught his disciples that to serve man is to serve god.

On the last day of his life, he taught Shukla-Yajurveda to his disciples at the Ramakrishna Mission, Belur Math. Swami Vivekananda obtained samadhi on 4 July 1902.

His ideas, however, live on in his works like *Raja Yoga*, *Karma Yoga*, *Bhakti Yoga* and *Jnana Yoga*. His birthday, 12 January, is celebrated as National Youth Day in India.

A Man with a Dream

Name: Nagavara Ramarao Narayana Murthy
Birth Date: 20 August 1946
Place: Mysore, Karnataka

On a chilly winter morning in 1990, five of the seven founders of a company met in their small office in a Bangalore suburb. The decision at hand was the possible sale of the company for an enticing sum of a million dollars.

For a while, one of the founders let his younger colleagues talk about their future plans. Discussions about the travails of their journey thus far and future challenges went on for hours. The founder did not utter a word.

Finally, it was his turn. He spoke about their journey from a small Bombay apartment in 1981—a passage beset with challenges—but also about how he believed they were in the darkest hour just before dawn. Then he made an audacious move. If they were all bent upon selling the company, he offered to buy them out. And this when he did not even have sufficient money to do so!

The room was stunned into silence. His colleagues wondered aloud about his foolhardiness. After an hour of arguments, he managed to convince them to change their minds to his way of thinking. He insisted that to create a great company, they would have to remain optimistic and confident. All the people in that room have more than lived up to their promise of that day.

The name of the optimist is Narayana Murthy, a software engineer and one of the founding members of Infosys Technologies, a consulting and information technology services company headquartered in India.

In the decades since that day, Infosys has grown to earn revenues in excess of three billion dollars, a net income of more than 800 million dollars and a market capitalization of over twenty-eight billion dollars, making it 28,000 times richer than the offer of one million dollars on that day.

In the process, Infosys has created more than 70,000 well-paying jobs, 2,000-plus dollar-millionaires and 20,000-plus rupee millionaires.

Born into a Kannada Madhwa Brahmin family in Mysore, Narayana Murthy graduated with a degree in electrical engineering from National Institute of Engineering, Mysore, in 1967 and then completed his post graduation from Indian Institute of Technology, Kanpur, in 1969. He has also been conferred with several honorary doctorates from universities across the world.

His wife Sudha Murthy is a social worker and a gifted writer. She is the inspiration in Narayana Murthy's life, the person who has stood by him in every difficulty and guided him through rough weather. They have two children, Rohan and Akshata.

Narayana Murthy served as the founder CEO of Infosys for twenty-one years until he retired at the age of sixty. He continues as the non-executive chairman of the board. He also serves on the boards of diverse other companies as well as global universities.

Narayana Murthy has been the recipient of numerous prestigious awards and honours. In 2008, he was awarded the Padma Vibhushan, the second highest civilian award by the Government of India, and Legion of honour, the highest civilian award awarded by France.

In 2010, in what is considered to be the highest professional distinction for an engineer, the American National Academy of Engineers elected Narayana Murthy as a foreign member. In 2011, he received the *Forbes* Lifetime Achievement Award. In 2012, *Fortune* magazine has named him one of the greatest entrepreneurs of our times. He is a great motivator of people. His credo, in his own words, is this: 'Performance leads to recognition. Recognition brings respect. Respect enhances power. Humility and grace in one's moments of power enhances dignity of an organization.'

The Emperor of Magic

Name: P. C. Sorcar
Birth Date: 23 February 1913
Place: Tangail, Bangladesh
Death Date: 6 January 1971
Place: Ashaikawa, Japan

Protul Chandra Sarkar's name has become synonymous with the world of fantasy. His showmanship was one of its kinds. He possessed the mastery to combine comedy, drama and mystery under one roof along with flamboyant aesthetics. With his uniquely styled maharaja costumes, spectacular sets, elaborate illusions, and exotic lighting, the magician enthralled audiences for hours as they kept asking for more.

Protul Chandra Sorcar, fondly called Jadusamrat or 'Emperor of Magic', was popular across the globe for his magic show called Indrajal. Sorcar demonstrated a completely new realm and proved that fantasy can exist. While performing marvellously intelligent tricks and unique feats, he challenged nature with an ease unthinkable for an average individual.

His singular devotion and dedication set him on the path of glory. His shows soon became international attractions and he garnered fans not only in India but also abroad. He surprised the French by cycling blindfolded in the Champs-Élysées and Place de l'Opera. In his popular feat named 'Water of India', one could enjoy the sight of water continuously flowing from a vessel throughout the show.

Born into a middle-class family in what is now Bangladesh, Sorcar was attracted to magic during his school days when he started performing in shows. He was a brilliant student and his extracurricular activities did not affect his academic performance. He graduated with honours in mathematics and then chose magic as his profession. He started the acclaimed All India Magic Circle and taught tricks to thousands of people who joined him.

Sorcar's illustrious career was not without obstacles. Critics challenged his potential and predicted his failure. He proved them wrong by attaining heights of success and charting an inspirational career graph. He is considered the 'Father of Indian Magic' and very rightly so.

Sorcar's wife, Basanti Devi, was the backbone of his phenomenal achievements. She not only assisted him in his profession but also brought up her five children while Sorcar went on long tours across the globe. She also contributed immensely backstage by designing the famous costumes he wore and also stitching the stage draperies. With her unconditional support, Sorcar reached new heights in the magical world. He contributed articles on magic to numerous magazines and newspapers and authored twenty-two books. His children also played instrumental roles by assisting their father on stage.

Sorcar died early while performing in a stage show at Japan. In 2010, the Indian government issued a postage stamp to commemorate the glory of this great magician who also received the prestigious Padma Shri.

Sorcar's tradition of magic is now carried forward by his sons. His oldest son, Manick, is famous for his laser shows and is also an acclaimed animator. His second son, Prodip, famed for his vanishing tricks, was named as the successor by the Jadusamrat himself. He carried forward the Indrajal show after his father's death with initial support from his brothers. Provas, the third son, is also a successful magician, as well as a ballet dancer and aviator. Thus, as they say, the show must go on.

Television Personality of the Millennium

Name: Prannoy Roy
Birth Date: 15 October 1949
Place: Calcutta, West Bengal

A familiar face with his salt and pepper beard, he is undisputedly, the brand equity of NDTV. With his background in chartered accountancy and economics, he was a newcomer in the genre of media and journalism. Yet, he brought in path-breaking transformation in news broadcasting with his simple, elegant and sophisticated presentation style.

Prannoy Roy successfully broke the stronghold that the government had until then on news broadcast and translated matters like the complicated election procedure into simple straightforward data that the common man, with an average educational background, could understand.

According to Prannoy, elections are more mathematical than mystical. With his popular exit polls using huge survey samples, he made savvy predictions

199

and, more often than not, hit the nail on its head, making the nation turn to him for his forecasts, irrespective of which political party finally clinched victory. Though he is a man of few words, he is a powerful author and commentator of current affairs whom the entire nation loves to listen to.

Roy showed a lot of interest in the political arena as well as elections even during his young age. He completed his higher studies in the UK and married his long-time friend Radhika before he came back to India in 1975. After a doctorate in economics, he dabbled between teaching, consulting assignments and election forecasting before he was offered the coveted post of an economic advisor in the finance ministry.

India was exposed to TV only in 1959 and the first colour TV came in only after 1982. At that time, news broadcasting was almost a monopoly in the states with no rivals. Private TV channels were banned. When Indian players were finally given a chance to reach the viewers, Prannoy foresaw that TV had a huge potential in the news market and wanted to make an impact by providing constant updates to the viewers.

With the efforts of Prannoy, his wife and a small team of producers and journalists, NDTV came into being in 1988. The team enjoyed their first breakthrough when they secured a prime slot on Doordarshan to host the popular news programme *The World This Week*. The reportage of the channel during important events like the fall of the Berlin Wall and Tiananmen Square created waves all over the nation winning the team a slot in the daily news bulletin. As their reputation grew, other well-known international TV channels looked upon NDTV to provide content about the Indian news scenario.

When the recognition and infrastructure slowly fell in place, NDTV managed to acquire a five-year contract with Star News. During the renewal of this successful contract, however, Star TV refused to give them full control over the editorial. Prannoy and Radhika then took the next logical step to start an independent news broadcasting channel. Infrastructure, credibility, financial backing, recognition, manpower—nothing was a major issue then. By April 2003, NDTV India and NDTV 24x7 went on air and gained instant acceptance among viewers. Very soon, they were among the top-rated English news channels.

Within a short period of going public, NDTV's share prices skyrocketed as it gained credibility among more than fifty million viewers who trusted its future potential.

Commanding over 30 per cent of the share of the English news market, NDTV is already a winner in its own rights, generating big revenues for its investors. The power couple, Prannoy and Radhika, hold more than half of its shares while some are owned by their daughter Tara. Prannoy is a more popular face, as he anchors the 9 p.m. news on NDTV three times a week while Radhika avoids media attention. She assists behind the scenes though and her contribution to establishing the channel's identity is phenomenal.

Strategies to build a network of local news channels by establishing collaborations with different states are in process. But the ultimate aim for the Roy couple is to look beyond the nation and establish an Indian standing in the global arena. The imprint of the red dot (resembling a *bindi*) in the logo and the inclusion of the tabla riff in the signature tune has given it an unmistakable Indianness.

Payyoli Express

Name: P.T. Usha
Birth Date: 27 June 1964
Place: Payyoli, Kerala

It was 1976. The Kerala government had just started a sports school for women. A twelve-year-old puny girl from Meladi, a small village near Calicut, was chosen to represent her district, Payyoli.

Though physically lean and unimpressive, the girl had amazing grit and determination. In 1979, when she participated in the National School Games, her athletic potential was noticed by coach O.M. Nambiar. Immensely confident that she would go places, he became her coach and remained so for the rest of her stint as an athlete.

Coming from a background where young girls were expected to stay at home, the 'Payyoli Express' dared to run. She participated in the Moscow Olympics in 1980 and shot into the limelight by winning two silver medals at the Delhi Asian Games in 1982. This was the start of a glorious career; collecting medals soon became a habit with her!

This Asian sprint queen is none other than Pilavullakandi Thekkeparambil Usha, known worldwide as P.T. Usha. A trendsetter, Usha broke all barriers and became a catalyst for many young girls to come out of their shells and prove their worth. She continues to be an inspiration for millions of sportswomen to take on all kinds of hurdles in their strides.

Usha is regarded as the queen of Indian tracks even today. She entered the athletic scene in a male-dominated era, when it was a rarity to see women in tracksuits. But nobody could stop her sprinting heels that were always on fire, ready to take up any challenge, which she did by systematic and rigorous training. Time and again, she proved her critics wrong as she forged ahead with confidence. Her perseverance took her to extraordinary heights and she evolved as one of India's most successful athletes.

Usha's career reached a pinnacle when she participated in the 1984 Olympics in Los Angeles. She became the first Indian woman to reach the finals of an Olympic event. It was also one of the saddest moments of her career as she lost the bronze by a hundredth of a second. However, she created an Indian national record, which is yet to be broken.

Another brilliant spell followed in the Asian Games at Seoul in 1986 when the 'Golden Girl' won four gold medals and a silver. For the next five years, the nation looked to her for bringing home name, fame and awards in athletics.

In 1991, when Usha married V. Srinivasan, she announced her retirement from sports. However, with strong support and encouragement from her husband, she made an amazing comeback seven years later and astonished the nation again by winning medals. At the age of thirty-four, Usha, then the mother of a boy, set a new national record in 200 metres race, silencing all questions about her decision to come back to the tracks.

Usha has won many accolades in her glorious career. A recipient of the Arjuna Award and the prestigious Padma Shri, she was also known as the 'Greatest Woman Athlete at the Asian Games'. She has also been named as 'Sportsperson of the Century' by the Indian Olympic Association. A road in Cochin has been named after her. Her biography is entitled *Golden Girl*.

Her brief break from athletic coaching brought down her fitness quotient considerably and she met with a couple of injuries. Usha finally announced her permanent retirement as an athlete in 2000. She now serves as an employee of Indian Railways. She also took a giant stride forward by announcing the establishment of the Usha School of Athletics to train young girls for national and international meets. The Payyoli Express is all set to nurture many more glorious Indian athletes.

The Renaissance Man

Name: Rabindranath Tagore
Birth Date: 7 May 1861
Place: Calcutta, West Bengal
Death Date: 7 August 1941
Place: Calcutta, West Bengal

A renowned and widely-travelled Indian poet, who inspired many other writers across continents as well, once took his unpublished poetic work to Charles Andrews, a literary expert and a protégé of Mahatma Gandhi. Andrews detected some grammatical flaws in the work and advised the poet to make certain changes. After the revisions, the poet approached the well known English writer W.B. Yeats to review his composition. Yeats felt that the poems were exceptional but pointed out the same corrected areas as ones that did not make authentic poetic sense and seemed to be in defiance with the innate nature of the poet's style! The Indian poet immediately realized what was wrong and reverted the lyrics to their original form.

Yeats went on to write the preface for the English translation of this composition, *Gitanjali (Song*

Offerings), one of the most famous poetic works of the author. The work was awarded the Nobel Prize for Literature in 1913 making the poet, Rabindranath Tagore, the first Asian to become a Nobel laureate.

Tagore, popularly called Gurudev, was born into a wealthy Brahmin family in Calcutta to Debendranath Tagore and Sarada Devi. His grandfather was a social reformer and the family lineage included the founders of the Adi Dharm faith.

As a child, Tagore disliked conventional education and received home tutoring. In 1873, he left Calcutta with his father to tour India, via his father's Santiniketan estate, and proceeding to the Himalayan hill station of Dalhousie. There, Tagore read biographies, studied history, astronomy, modern science, Sanskrit and examined the classical poetry of Kalidasa. This trip laid the foundation for Tagore's inclination towards literature.

By the age of eight, Tagore was already writing and publishing poetry anonymously. At sixteen, he published under the pseudonym Bhanushingho ('Sun Lion') and also wrote short stories and plays. His first book of poems, *Kabi Kahini* ('Tale of a Poet') was published in 1878.

At seventeen, he went to England for formal schooling and briefly studied law. However, he soon detached himself from conventional education to explore diverse subjects like Shakespeare and folk music and eventually returned without a degree to Bengal in

1880. Then he made a career as a poet and writer. His works, which depicted a wide range of urban and rural subjects, earned him a large following. *Galpaguchchha* is a collection of stories about poverty in Bengal while *Manasi, Naivedya* and *Kheya* are noted works of poetry. *Gora, Shesher Kobita* and *Chaturanga* are some of his reputed novels.

Tagore wrote over 2,000 songs, collectively now popular as Rabindra Sangeet. They were based on Indian classical music and folk music and later collected into a book called *Gitabitan*. He is the only individual to have penned the national anthems of two countries: *Jana gana mana* for India and *Amar shonar bangla* for Bangladesh.

In 1905, when Lord Curzon decided to partition Bengal, Tagore strongly protested via songs and meetings. He introduced the Rakhi Bandhan ceremony, symbolizing the underlying unity of undivided Bengal.

He established an experimental school at Santiniketan, based on the pattern of Indian ashrams. The foundation for the Visva-Bharati school, which employed gurus to provide individualized guidance to pupils, was laid on 22 December 1918. It grew into Visva-Bharati University.

In 1915, Tagore was knighted by King George V. Four years later, following the Jallianwala Bagh massacre, Tagore renounced his knighthood. Tagore supported Gandhi but stayed out of politics and did not hesitate to oppose Gandhiji on views that he found inappropriate.

Apart from poetry, literature and music, Tagore was a keen observer of Western culture, and had a good grasp of modern physics as well. He held his own in a debate even with Einstein in 1930 on the newly emerging principles of quantum mechanics and chaos. His exploration of biology, physics, and astronomy impacted his poetry as well while his essays spoke with conviction about political and personal issues. He also wrote plays like *Visarjan, Chandalika, Dak Ghar* and *Raktakarabi* and even acted in some of his own productions. Many of his writings have inspired film adaptations such as *Chokher Bali* and *Ghare Baire*.

Tagore travelled extensively and shared his views with many noteworthy contemporaries like Einstein, Robert Frost, George Bernard Shaw, H.G. Wells, Benito Mussolini, and Yeats.

In 1940, Oxford University awarded Tagore with a Doctor of Literature. Till the end, Tagore criticized orthodoxy, denounced communalism, spoke his mind with conviction and did not hesitate to share his views. He passed away after an extended illness on 7 August 1941 at his home in Calcutta. However, to quote his own words, 'Death is not extinguishing the light; it is only putting out the lamp because the dawn has come.'

Although Tagore is one of the greatest representatives of India, his life and works encompass much more than his country. He was truly a man who belonged to the entire world, a product of the best of both traditional Indian and modern Western cultures.

The Master Artist

Name: Raja Ravi Varma
Birth Date: 29 April 1848
Place: Travancore, Kerala
Death Date: 2 October 1906
Place: Travancore, Kerala

Raja Ravi Varma, a painter of great repute, once asked the Maharaja of Udaipur to pose for a portrait. When the Maharaja said he could not take time out from his busy schedule, Ravi Varma requested him to spare at least half an hour so he could note down his dimensions. Once this was done, the artist took leave, only requesting access to the royal robes so that he could replicate them on canvas. In three days, the artist delivered an impeccable portrait. Since the Maharaja hadn't had time to pose for the portrait, Ravi Varma had created it with a mental image as reference. The Maharaja was both impressed and elated. Such was Ravi Varma's skill as a painter.

His talent was first discovered by his uncle Raja Raja Varma. When Ravi Varma was just a little boy, he would often draw on the walls of his home as many children do. However, his pictures of animals and events of daily life captured the interest of his uncle, who recognized the signs of a remarkable talent. A painter himself, he took on the role of formally training Ravi Varma.

This training process took a significant step forward when, at the age of fourteen, Ravi Varma was sent to the Kilimanoor Palace in Thiruvananthapuram, to receive instruction under the tutelage of the palace painter Rama Swamy Naidu. Naidu honed Ravi Varma's skill in working with watercolours. While at the palace, Ravi Varma also received immense encouragement from the king himself, Ayilyam Thirunal, who was a great patron of the arts.

Ravi Varma also learnt much from the Dutch painter Theodor Jensen, who had come to the palace to paint portraits of the royal family. This phase saw Ravi Varma move to oil paintings.

The blend of Indian and Western influences in Ravi Varma's paintings can be attributed to the distinctive methods used by his two teachers.

Ravi Varma gained international recognition in 1873, when he won the first place at the Vienna Art Exhibition. He is best known for his paintings depicting scenes from the Ramayana and the Mahabharata, the great Indian epics. He is also known for the fact that his paintings depicted women in an exquisite manner that found much appreciation even in foreign countries. Towards the latter part of his life, his paintings also began to reflect aspects of folk life and culture.

Shakuntala, Lord Rama Conquers Varuna, Draupadi Dreading to Meet Kichaka, Damayanti Talking to a Swan, A Family of Beggars, Lady Lost in Thought, and *The Heartbroken* are some of his best known works.

At one point, Ravi Varma travelled the length and breadth of India in search of new subjects, and many of his paintings of common life were inspired by what he observed on these journeys. Ravi Varma had a reputation for being a great portrait artist, and received frequent requests from members of royal families all over India to have their portraits made by him.

Ravi Varma is said to be one of the pioneers in launching art as an enterprise. He made several prints of his original works and distributed them commercially, making them affordable for the public at large. A prolific artist, he is said to have painted over 7,000 pictures in his lifetime.

A college in Kerala and a school in Kilimanoor are named after this great painter. The Hindi movie *Rang Rasiya* (2008) and the Malayalam film *Makaramanju* (2010) are inspired by his life and work. In recognition of his phenomenal contribution to Indian art, the Government of Kerala has set up an award, the Raja Ravi Varma Puraskaram, for individuals who show remarkable promise in the field of art and culture.

Indian in Space

Name: Rakesh Sharma
Birth Date: 13 January 1949
Place: Patiala, Punjab

He holds the credit of being the first Indian (and the 138th person) to step into space. In 1984, he completed his eight-day mission away from Earth, along with colleagues, and returned to a hero's welcome.

He was awarded the Ashok Chakra by the Indian government. The government of the erstwhile Soviet Union also honoured him with 'The Order of Lenin' and the 'Hero of Soviet Union' award, the highest Russian honour.

Born to a Brahmin family in Punjab and schooled at Hyderabad, Rakesh enrolled at the National Defence Academy in 1966. Graduating three years later, he joined the Indian Air Force. In the two years that followed, Rakesh gained credibility and proved his talent through his flying assignments, thereby rapidly rising through the ranks.

When the Soviet Union collaborated with the Indian Space Research Programme in 1980 and offered to include an Indian in its spacecraft, two Indian Air Force pilots were selected. One of them was Rakesh Sharma, then a squadron leader. Along with Ravish Malhotra, his colleague who was a wing commander, Rakesh underwent rigorous training for eighteen months in Moscow. The programme included a yoga regimen to keep them fit and healthy enough to travel into space!

While Rakesh was India's primary candidate for this prestigious assignment, Ravish was prepared as a back up. Both pilots were kept in an equal state of readiness until twenty-four hours before the flight. Finally, squadron leader Rakesh accompanied another wing commander and flight engineer from the Soviet Union. The whole world awaited the outcome of this brave mission.

Rakesh boarded the spacecraft Soyuz T-11 on 3 April 1984 along with his overseas colleagues and it powered off from Kazakhstan. The team had a successful rendezvous with the orbiting laboratory in space, Salyut 7. During their eight-day tenure aboard this laboratory, they conducted thirteen challenging experiments in the fields of material and biomedical sciences in outer space. When the team returned successfully, they had captured valuable photographs in addition to bringing back matter from outer space. Through multi-spectral photography, Rakesh captured parts of northern India at a time when hydroelectric power stations were about to be launched in the picturesque Himalayan regions. This was a valuable contribution by the first Indian cosmonaut to explore space.

Following his extraordinary journey, Rakesh Sharma worked as chief test pilot for many decades and retired as a Wing Commander in 2001. He has been a part of many prestigious and challenging projects like the Jet Trainer Project and the Light Combat Aircraft Project at Hindustan Aeronautics Ltd (Nasik and Bangalore divisions).

After his historic space flight, the then prime minister Indira Gandhi asked Rakesh Sharma how India looked from up there. The squadron leader replied with conviction, 'Sare jahan se achcha!'

The Relentless Reformer

Name: Ram Mohan Roy
Born: 22 May 1772
Place: Murshidabad, West Bengal
Death Date: 27 September 1833
Place: Bristol, England

It was a shocking day for the young man. He had tried, in vain, to persuade his sister-in-law not to immolate herself on his brother's funeral pyre. When she felt the touch of the flames, she started screaming and attempted to escape but relatives and priests forced her back on to the pyre. Her agonized shrieks were drowned out by the loud beating of drums. There and then, he resolved not to rest until the barbaric custom of sati had been wiped out of India.

He also laid the foundation for India's great future without giving up on what was good and noble in the Indian way of life. He was hailed as the 'Maker of Modern India' as he made significant contributions to the evolution of the nation.

One of the greatest social reformers that India has produced, Ram Mohan Roy was born into a wealthy, conservative Brahmin family in Bengal. His father, Ramakanta Roy, was a devout Hindu who rigorously performed his religious duties. Ram Mohan was devoted to Lord Vishnu in his early childhood. So much so, he decided to become a monk when he was fourteen but his mother, Tarini Devi, who was a worshipper of divine feminine power, persuaded him not to. He was sent to Patna for higher studies and, by the age of fifteen, he had learnt Bengali, Persian, Arabic and Sanskrit.

He acquainted himself with Western philosophy and literature and read widely to gain first-hand knowledge of Islam, Sufism and Buddhism. He studied Hindu scriptures in detail to comprehend the real spirit of the religion. He concluded that some people, for their own selfish ends, had mutilated religious beliefs; real Hinduism was very different from what was being practised in society. He actively denounced idol worship and set his mind to work towards religious reform.

Ram Mohan Roy also advocated reforms in education and stressed the need for modern education in order to bring about national progress. He was in favour of a scientific approach to education to effect socio-economic change. He helped the British government promote a more liberal system of learning, including subjects like English, mathematics, chemistry and anatomy. He believed that a new education system would liberate India from the shackles of superstitions and usher in social reforms.

As a social reformer, one of Roy's greatest achievements was in convincing the British to abolish sati. Shaken to the core by the incident in his own family, he worked relentlessly by writing, petitioning and organizing vigilance committees to do away with this inhuman practice. In 1820, his article 'A Second Conference between an Advocate for, and An Opponent of the Practice of Burning Widows Alive' was published. It proved that the custom of sati was a case of misrepresentation of Hindu law. His efforts paid off when Lord William Bentinck then governer-general passed a law in 1829, banning the practice of sati.

Ram Mohan Roy did not stop there. He justified the remarriage of widows, strove against child marriage, and worked to restore the dignity of socially downtrodden women. He also engaged himself in literary pursuits focusing on translating works from Sanskrit to Bengali and writing essays on subjects concerning religion.

He is considered the pioneer of modern Indian journalism. He started the Bengali weekly *Sambad Kaumudi* ('The Moon of Intelligence') and Persian weekly *Mirat-ul-Akhbar* ('Mirror of News'), which were successful in awakening the masses to the cultural and political ideas of the West. In 1825, he founded the Vedanta College where students were taught Vedanta philosophy along with Western science and philosophy.

Ram Mohan Roy was the first man to translate the

Vedanta into Bengali. He preached the theory that 'God is One' and stood for universal brotherhood. In 1828, along with other like-minded individuals, he founded Brahmo Sabha, which later came to be known as Brahmo Samaj. Through this reformist movement, he wanted to expose religious orthodoxy and hypocrisy and check the growing influence of Christianity on Hindu society. In 1830, the Emperor of Delhi, Akbar II, bestowed the title of 'Raja' to Ram Mohan Roy.

Raja Ram Mohan Roy visited England both as an ambassador of the Emperor and also to ensure that the ban on sati was not overturned. He died of meningitis at Stapleton in Bristol in 1833 during his visit to England.

Subhas Chandra Bose once said of him: 'Raja Ram Mohan Roy stands out against the dawn of the new awakening in India as the prophet of the new age.'

Bearer of the Spiritual Mace

Name: Ramakrishna Paramhamsa
Birth Date: 1836
Place: Kamarpukur, West Bengal
Death Date: 1886
Place: Cossipore, West Bengal

In the quiet village of Kamarpukur, a poor Brahmin called Khudiram Chattopadhyay decided to make a pilgrimage to Gaya. On reaching this holy place, he had a dream in which Lord Vishnu said, 'I will be born as your son.' At the same time, his wife Chandra Devi had a vision of giving birth to a divine child. When the child was born, they named him Gadadhar ('mace bearer'), an epithet of Vishnu. The child went on to become the spiritual guru, Ramakrishna Paramhamsa.

Gadadhar grew up into a remarkably intelligent boy with a remarkable memory. He would listen to stories from the Hindu epics and later recount or enact them for his friends and villagers. He had a creative bent of mind too. He mastered the art of pottery and learnt to paint as well.

Gadadhar had his first mystical experience when he was just seven years old. It was monsoon, and he was walking along the paddy fields munching puffed rice. Something made him look up and he saw a dangerous-looking thunder cloud enveloping the sky. As it spread rapidly, a flight of white cranes suddenly appeared just below it. Gadadhar was so overwhelmed by the sight that he fell to the ground, unconscious. Later, he told his parents and villagers about experiencing an indescribable ecstasy at that sight.

When Gadadhar was nine, his father passed away. The boy came to realize that life on earth is not permanent. The more he was convinced of the transitory nature of worldly things, the more he wanted to realize God.

Even as a child, he was interested in religion and India's spiritual heritage. He believed that all human beings are equal. So much so, that during his investiture ceremony (to become a practising Brahmin), he shocked everyone by accepting *prasad* from a low-caste woman. As he grew older, his spirituality deepened. He often lost himself in meditation and mystical musing.

When he was sixteen, his brother Ramkumar summoned him to Dakshineswar to assist him in priestly duties. However, mere rituals did not interest Gadadhar. He protested, 'Brother, what shall I do with mere breadwinning education? I'd rather acquire that wisdom which will illumine my heart and give me satisfaction forever.'

In 1856, after Ramkumar breathed his last, Gadadhar had to become the priest at Dakshineswar temple to Goddess Kali. This temple had been built by a pious lady, Rani Rasmoni. Here, he meditated tirelessly in a sacred grove of five trees on the edge of the temple grounds seeking a vision of Goddess Kali or the Divine Mother. But the vision eluded him. He was so frustrated that he wanted to give up his life. Just then Goddess Kali appeared before him. That was the first of his numerous visions of the Divine Mother.

Soon, devotees started seeking him out for his religious views. People arrived from far and wide to listen to his discourses. His divine personality and magnetic style of presenting his thoughts drew multitudes to him, irrespective of age, creed or gender. People were greatly impressed with his purity, guilelessness, truthfulness and holiness. They felt an uplifting and sublime influence in his presence.

In 1861, a nun, Bhairavi Brahmani, appeared at Dakshineswar and initiated Ramakrishna into Tantra yoga and meditation. He acknowledged Tantra as a valid path to realizing God and it aided him in further spiritual growth. If Ramakrishna looked upon Brahmani as his mother, Brahmani considered him to be an incarnation of the divine.

Again, in 1864, a wandering monk named Totapuri arrived in Dakshineswar and taught Ramakrishna the path of Advaita Vedanta to realize God. Ramakrishna experienced a deep form of trance called *nirvikalpa samadhi* under his guidance. According to Saradananda Maharaj, a direct disciple of Ramakrishna, this was the time he came to be known as Shri Ramakrishna Paramhamsa. Paramhamsa, literally 'supreme swan', also stands for 'supreme soul who is one with God'— one who has attained enlightenment.

Ramakrishna did not want to start a cult. He did not show a new path to salvation. His message was 'realization of god'. His message was exclusive in that it had universal appeal. He preached the universality of religion and promoted individuality in the seeker's approach to god. His principal teachings are as follow:

- **See God in all:** God is in the form of the saint, God is in the form of the sinner, God is in the form of the righteous, God is in the form of the unrighteous.
- **God is within you:** I see Him as all. Men and other creatures appear to me only as hollow forms, moving their heads and hands and feet, but within is the Lord Himself.
- **Persevere in search of God:** There are pearls in the deep sea, but one must hazard all to find them. If diving once does not bring you pearls, dive again and again. You are sure to be rewarded in the end. So is it. So if your first attempt with the finding of the Lord in this world proves fruitless, do not lose heart. Persevere in your efforts. You are sure to realize him at last.
- **Trust completely in God:** Give up everything to Him, resign yourself to Him, and there will be

no more trouble for you. Then you will come to know that everything is done by his will.

- **Love of God is essential:** Undiluted love of God is the essential thing. All else is unreal.

Ramakrishna Paramhamsa died of cancer in 1886. His wife Sharada Devi, a saint in her own right, took charge of his disciples and carried on his message.

Ramakrishna's chief disciple, Swami Vivekananda, promoted a more activist form of Hinduism. He showed to the world that Hindu religion was also valuable as far as improving the society was concerned. He also worked towards the establishment of the Ramakrishna Math and Mission, which has centres spread across the world today.

Showman of Bollywood

Name: Ranbir Raj Kapoor
Birth Date: 14 December 1924
Place: Peshawar (now Pakistan)
Death Date: 2 June 1988
Place: Bombay, Maharashtra

It was a time when the world was not as connected as it is today. High achievers were recognized in their own countries but not as well known globally. Yet the work of some artists had the power to transcend national barriers and win them worldwide admiration.

One such artist was once travelling from India to Moscow. His son, who generally accompanied him, had forgotten their travel documents at the immigration counter in Delhi. Just before they were to land in Moscow, the son realized his folly. The captain of the Air India flight duly informed Moscow traffic control that the artist would not be able to alight in the Soviet capital because he had misplaced his passport. Yet, when the plane reached Moscow, a red carpet had been laid out up to the door of the aircraft. Within seconds,

Soviet officials hopped aboard and escorted the artist out with all respect, saying, 'One of his stature needs no visa or passport to enter the Soviet Union.' Such was the love that Russia and many other nations of the world held in their hearts for the showman of Indian cinema—Raj Kapoor.

Born Ranbir Raj Kapoor, he received film-making as an inheritance from his father Prithviraj Kapoor. It was to become a family legacy as it travelled from him and his brothers to their children and grandchildren. Raj was the eldest of six children of whom two others, Shashi and Shammi, also went on to become great actors of their times.

Raj appeared in his debut film *Inquilab* at the age of eleven when his father's friend Kidar Sharma gave him a break. The director figured that the boy, who had been sent by his father to assist him on the sets, was more interested in working in front of the camera!

Twelve years later, in 1947, the aspiring actor got his big break opposite Madhubala in *Neel Kamal*. A year later, aged twenty-four, he established RK Studios, becoming the youngest director of the time. In the same year, he made *Aag* with Nargis, who went on to become his favourite co-star. When Nargis married actor Sunil Dutt, Raj is said to have suffered a major setback. But all the experiences of his life eventually became his inspiration for cinema, so he continued making movies that reflected life as he saw it—beautiful and full of love. His movies depicted love in all its forms, from patriotic to sensual, from teen romances to love triangles.

Raj Kapoor produced, directed and starred in many box office hits such as *Barsaat* (1949), *Awaara* (1951), *Shree 420* (1955), *Chori Chori* (1956) and *Jis Desh Mein Ganga Behti Hai* (1960). He also came to be known as 'The Tramp', as he modelled his screen persona on Charlie Chaplin's famous role.

After World War II, given the circumstances of social insecurity and economic strain, many people across the globe identified with his character from *Awara*. The movie brought him international fame in countries like Iran, Turkey, China and the former Soviet Union. *Shri 420* was another film of the same genre that brought hope to many. Most of his movies presented the common man who always won in the end. Hence they appealed to the masses.

In 1964, he produced, directed and starred in *Sangam*, his first film in colour. Shot in exotic locations across Europe, it showcased a glamorous lifestyle so characteristic of Raj's own.

Mera Naam Joker in 1970 reinvented the tramp as the circus clown. This was Raj's most expensive and ambitious film and also his most long-drawn production. He brought to India an entire Russian circus and a ballerina to star in the film. The film traced the struggle and the sorrow of the life of a jester, who himself bears pain in life and yet spreads happiness and laughter around. The film was a huge flop in its time but went on to become a success many years later. Raj Kapoor suffered a major setback emotionally and financially because of this flop. However, not a man to give up, he reinvented himself yet again and returned to the audiences in 1971 with *Kal Aaj Aur Kal*, co-starring with his elder son Randhir Kapoor. This was followed in 1973 by *Bobby*, in which he introduced his younger son Rishi Kapoor as well as actress Dimple Kapadia. Raj Kapoor introduced many new artists, and several of them went on to make a mark for themselves in the Indian film industry.

The film-maker was a great believer in teamwork. He had his own panel of writers, Shailendra and Hasrat Jaipuri; his regular singers, Mukesh and Lata Mangeshkar, and his favourite composers, Shankar Jaikishen. On Mukesh's death, he is known to have lamented, 'I have lost my voice today.'

Always a stickler for perfection, Raj Kapoor would spend hours with all his co-stars and artists, untiring till he got things done the way he wanted them. He was always open to learning though; his cabinet contained endless clippings of articles on film-making from all over the world. His life revolved around cinema.

Kapoor received many awards throughout his career, including nine Filmfare Awards and nineteen nominations. The Government of India honoured him with the Padma Bhushan in 1971 and the Dadasaheb Phalke Award, the highest award for cinematic excellence in India, in 1987. In 2001, he was honoured as the Best Director of the Millennium by *Stardust*. He was named 'Showman of the Millennium' at the Star Screen Awards in 2002.

It was in 1988 when he was due to receive the Dadasaheb Phalke Award from President R. Venkataraman that Raj Kapoor started experiencing discomfort. Soon, he breathed his last. At the time of his death, he was working on a film called *Henna*. Later completed by his son Randhir, it became a phenomenal hit—a fitting tribute to the legacy of Raj Kapoor, the showman.

Rani of Jhansi

Name: Rani Lakshmi Bai
Birth Date: 19 November 1835
Place: Benaras, British India
Death Date: 18 June 1858
Place: Gwalior, British India

Two young men and a young girl were racing their horses on the bank of the Ganges. The girl surged ahead. One of the men tried to overtake her but his horse stumbled and he fell off the horse.

'O Manu, I am dead!' he cried. With great difficulty, the girl lifted him and made him sit on her horse. With help from the other young man, they reached the palace. The injured youth was Nana Saheb, adopted son of Baji Rao, the Peshwa of the Maratha Empire. The girl was Manikarnika, daughter of the courtier Moropanth.

Moropanth saw them and said, 'Manu, how unfortunate! Nana is seriously hurt.'

'No father, he's hurt just a little. Didn't Abhimanyu continue to fight although he was seriously injured?'

'Those times were different, Manu.'

'What is the difference, father? It is the same sky, the same earth, the same sun, the same moon.'

'But Manu, the fortunes of the country have changed. This is the age of the British. We are powerless before them.'

Moropanth's reasoning didn't convince the brave little Manu. How could a future queen, Rani Lakshmi Bai of Jhansi, be expected to agree with such a lame argument?

Lakshmi Bai was born as Manikarnika (nicknamed Manu) to Moropanth and Bhagirathi Bai. She lost her mother at the tender age of four and was raised by her father. Along with her studies, she was given formal training in horsemanship, shooting and fencing. She turned out to be a beauty with brains.

Manikarnika was married at the age of fourteen to Raja Gangadhar Rao, Maharaja of Jhansi. Manikarnika became Rani Lakshmi Bai, Queen of Jhansi. In 1951, she gave birth to a son who unfortunately died when he was only four months old. After his death, the couple adopted a child legally with the local British authorities as witness and named him Damodar Rao. Gangadhar passed away in 1853 when Lakshmi Bai was just eighteen.

After his death, the British rulers refused to accept Damodar Rao as the legal heir. Lord Dalhousie decided to seize the state of Jhansi as per the Doctrine of Lapse. The British confiscated the state jewels and wealth, and asked Lakshmi Bai to leave the Jhansi fort and go on pension. Rani Laksmi Bai refused—she was firm about protecting her people and her state.

Meanwhile, unrest started spreading in India and the British shifted their attention towards curbing rebellion. Jhansi was left undisturbed for a while. Seizing this opportunity, the Rani began forming a volunteer army. She provided military training to both men and women and prepared them to participate in the freedom movement.

In 1858, the British troops, led by General Hugh Rose, laid siege on Jhansi. With Damodar strapped to her back in order to keep her hands free, Lakshmi Bai led her army into a fierce battle. Unfortunately, her forces could not hold out long. In two weeks, the British captured the city.

Lakshmi Bai fled to Kalpi along with her son and some warriors. There she joined other rebel forces including those of Tatya Tope. They moved on to Gwalior to continue their fight for the independence of India. In 1858, she died in the battle to save Gwalior fort. She was only twenty-two.

Rani of Jhansi became an icon of the Indian Independence movement owing to her courage, wisdom, and progressive views on women's empowerment. She was a brave queen who sacrificed her life for her nation. Statues of this indomitable patriot on horseback are found across India. Several novels have been based on her life and her legend has been captured in films like *The Tiger and the Flame* and *The Rebel*.

Maestro of the Strings

Name: Ravi Shankar
Birth Date: 7 April 1920
Place: Benaras, British India

Ustad Allauddin Khan was not only a brilliant guru but also a tough taskmaster. Once, he was teaching his student Ravi Shankar a particularly complex composition. The student was unable to grasp the notes, and he grew furious. He severely criticized the way Ravi Shankar was playing the instrument. The student stormed out of the room in anger and began to pack his clothes, ready to leave the gurukul. A little later, however, the teacher came in and embraced the student and the student realized, in turn, that it would be foolish to turn away from such a mentor.

Such was the relationship that Pandit Ravi Shankar, the man who went on to become a renowned sitar maestro, shared with his guru. Speaking of it much later in a television interview, he stated that his guru had been more like a father to him, and had provided him with training so unique that it helped him make his mark not only in India but also in the global arena.

Born in Benaras to a well-off and educated Bengali family, Ravi Shankar's birth name was Robindro Shaunkor Chowdhury. His father was a barrister in London. His brother Uday Shankar was an accomplished choreographer. Ravi Shankar first became acquainted with the world outside India at the age of ten when he started travelling with his brother's dance troupe and eventually participating in the performances. During his foreign tours, he became familiar with Western music, languages and culture.

By the time he was fifteen, he had met Ustad Allauddin Khan through his brother. Ustadji was then travelling as part of the troupe for a year. During that period, he coached Ravi Shankar intermittently and also introduced him to the sitar.

It was not long before Ravi Shankar made up his mind to train under the Ustad, even if it meant going back to India and forsaking his future in dance. When he was eighteen, he moved to Maihar in Madhya Pradesh, to become part of the Ustad's gurukul. As a student, he was often required to practise for fourteen hours in a day, and his training continued in this manner for another six years, although he had started performing in public much earlier.

He then moved to Bombay and started composing music with the Indian People's Theatre Association. He also worked briefly with All India Radio. What is notable from this period of Ravi Shankar's life is that he composed a new rendition of the national song *Saare jahaan se acchan.* He also composed the music for Satyajit Ray's internationally acclaimed Apu trilogy.

During the latter half of the 1950s, Ravi Shankar began touring and performing for international audiences in the UK, the US and Europe. *Three Ragas* (1956) was one of his earliest albums. His music stirred the minds of many, including George Harrison of The Beatles. Harrison came to India in 1966 to learn the sitar from him. Thus began a long and fruitful collaboration that boosted Ravi Shankar's career.

Ravi Shankar has been credited with popularizing Indian classical music in the West. Besides winning the Grammy Award three times, he has been nominated for an Oscar for his music score in the film *Gandhi*. He has also been awarded the Padma Bhushan, Padma Vibhushan, Bharat Ratna and the Ramon Magsaysay Award. His autobiography *My Music, My Life*, was published in 1968, followed by another memoir entitled *Raga Mala*.

Being a person who holds music in high esteem, Ravi Shankar has often spoken out against audiences that are disrespectful or inattentive during concerts. Referring to his music, he has said that although he is not much of a speaker otherwise, he can speak through his sitar and that is how he is able to effectively express all his feelings. He still gives recitals, often accompanied by his daughter Anoushka.

First Lady of Fashion

Name: Ritu Beri
Birth Date: 3 May, 1967
Place: Indore, Madhya Pradesh

This graduate from National Institute of Fashion Technology (NIFT) redefined style statements with her original and striking designs. She delighted Parisians by intelligently marketing creations which blended Mughal motifs with luxurious silks. These won her instant critical acclaim in an era when the Indian fashion industry could not think beyond certain accepted design patterns. She surprised her critics with every new creation, gracefully overlapping Indian and Western styles.

French connoisseurs were quick to recognize her talent and she became the first Asian to spearhead Scherer, the popular French brand. She is also the only Indian to be featured in acclaimed fashion magazine *Acustyl*. Often called the 'First Lady of Fashion', she is considered a prime driving force in bringing global recognition to Indian fashion.

Ritu Beri, the dynamic and versatile designer, has

worked wonders with colours, innovative textures, patterns and shapes in her illustrious career. She knows the pulse of every generation and creates funky and chic apparel that become a rage. Her designs are not necessarily jazzy or flamboyant. In fact, it is her intricate patterns that attract her fans.

After graduating from the University of Delhi, Ritu was on the lookout for some artistic challenge to channelize her creativity. She chose the path of fashion designing and started creating outfits for herself and her friends. Before she realized it, she had already made a modest beginning as a businesswoman.

Ritu strategically planned the changes that she wanted to bring into the fashion industry in order to stand apart from her contemporaries. She enrolled in NIFT and became one of the first twenty-five graduates of this now very prestigious institute. Equipped with the knowledge of trends and the skills of fashion designing, she confidently came up with her first collection, Lavanya, which enjoyed stupendous success in the Indian and global markets. This paved the way for her next experimental collection, Sanskriti, which reflected India's rich cultural heritage. Her collections delighted Indians and won her instant recognition in her homeland.

Later, she was given the challenging opportunity of designing the outfits of the Indian contingent for the curtain-raiser ceremony at the Atlanta Olympics. Apart from her stint in international events, she has enjoyed prestigious Indian assignments like designing uniforms for Delhi Police and for the staff at Hotel Hyatt Regency.

Some of her celebrated clients include Bill Clinton, Nicole Kidman, Prince Charles, Elizabeth Jagger, Andie MacDowell, Jerry Hall, Laetitia Casta, and the Swarovski family. Indians who wear her label include Preity Zinta, Madhuri Dixit, Rani Mukerji, and Parmeshwar Godrej.

Ritu's journey has been quite eventful, replete with frustrations and triumphs, criticisms and praises, stupendous successes and miserable failures. Apart from being a successful fashion designer, this multitalented personality is also an acclaimed columnist in many journals and has authored the popular book titled *101 Ways to Look Good*. Another of her works is *Firefly: A Fairytale*, a limited edition book, which she has published herself.

Ritu symbolizes the modern woman who balances professional and personal life with ease. She is married to an industrialist and is the proud mother of a six-year-old girl. A stunning beauty herself, Ritu is on NIFT's board of governors. She is also socially conscious and is involved in several charity initiatives. She is the honorary patron of Savera, an organization working for the betterment of women. Her compassion for animals has made her initiate the 'Caring Means Sharing' project to raise funds for animal care centres.

Creator of 'The Common Man'

Name: R.K. Laxman
Birth Date: 24 October 1921
Place: Mysore, Karnataka

He is considered a national treasure on account of his illustrations brimming with satire and humour. Fondly referred to as the 'Shakespeare of Indian Cartooning', this humourist has made his fans smile almost every morning with his witty newspaper series of sketches titled 'You Said It' featuring, The Common Man.

Rasipuram Krishnaswamy Laxman was the youngest in his family of six siblings. His father passed away when he was young but his schooling was not affected. Influenced by the illustrations that appeared in popular magazines like *Wide World*, *Bystander* and *Punch*, Laxman, the child, began to draw funny caricatures all over his house using chalk. He was also influenced by the works of British cartoonist Sir David Low. When Laxman finally took up cartooning as a profession, he imparted innovative humorous features to almost every character he drew.

In those times, cartoonists had hardly any opportunity to showcase their talent and pursue it as their profession but Laxman was determined to write his destiny on his own terms. His brother R.K. Narayan, the famous novelist, also played a major role in encouraging him to pursue his passion and creativity. Even before Narayan started working, Laxman developed illustrations for some stories written by his brother. Laxman's brilliance and spontaneity reflect in his illustrations for Narayan's *Malgudi Days* series.

Interestingly, Laxman and Narayan had completely contrasting personalities and temperaments. While Narayan was patient, gentle and reticent, Laxman was known for his antics, impish sense of humour and hyperactivity. Yet, the brothers maintained a close relationship throughout their lives even as they nurtured their individual careers according to their independent inclinations.

Laxman's cartoons initially appeared in magazines like *Swarajya*, *Blitz* and *Korvanji* (Kannada). The turning point came when he finally joined the *Times of India*. For more than fifty years, Laxman meticulously sets to work at 8.30 a.m. every day, unmindful of the bustling environment around him. He is the only journalist who has undisputedly interpreted almost every major event in India via meaningful sketches.

Laxman's creation, The Common Man, gained him lot of acclaim and fame. This character provided the unique voice in his sketches. He considers this signature character—with his ever-raised eyebrows, bald head, wisp of hair at his back, striped coat, spectacles perched on his bulbous nose—to be his best companion.

His notable collections include *Brushing Up The Years—A Cartoonist's History of India: 1947 to the Present*, *The Eloquent Brush: A Selection of Cartoons from Nehru to Rajiv*, and *50 Years of Independence Through the Eyes of R.K. Laxman*. His autobiography in English is entitled *The Tunnel of Time* while the Marathi version is titled *Lakshmanrekha*.

With his brilliant wit and tact, Laxman has gathered millions of fans around the world. He is the proud recipient of honours like Padma Bhushan, Padma Vibhushan, Ramon Magsaysay Award, and B.D. Goenka Award for his priceless contribution to the field of journalism. In recognition of his achievements, a special commemorative stamp of 'The Common Man' was released in India in 1988. *R.K. Laxman Ki Duniya* is a comedy TV series based on his works, featuring incidents in the life of The Common Man as portrayed over the years.

In 2003, Laxman suffered a stroke and the left side of his body was paralysed. However, his originality and innovation did not diminish as he continued to work from home. He faced multiple strokes in 2010 and was in a critical condition but finally managed to recover.

Laxman has carved a niche for himself with his powerful strokes on paper. He never fails to surprise people, age and nationality notwithstanding, with his witty interpretations of life.

The Maker of Malgudi

Name: R.K. Narayan
Birth Date: 10 October 1906
Place: Madras, British India
Death Date: 13 May 2001
Place: Chennai, Tamil Nadu

As a young man, Rasipuram Krishnaswami Iyer Narayanaswami was once visiting his sister in Coimbatore, when he chanced to meet a girl in the neighbourhood. He hadn't yet made his mark as a writer but he was determined to marry this girl. The girl's father was not too keen as the horoscopes of the couple didn't match. However, Narayan managed to convince him and soon married Rajam. He then took up a job with a Madras-based publication to support himself and his wife. In time, they had a daughter, Hemavathi. When the daughter was about three years old, tragedy befell Narayan. His beloved wife died of typhoid. Narayan was distraught. His highly acclaimed autobiographical novel *The English Teacher* chronicles his deep anguish. Narayan never remarried.

Despite being the son of a school teacher, Narayan

was never very good at studies. He genuinely loved reading though. His earliest works, *Swami and Friends* and *The Bachelor of Arts,* provide glimpses of his experiences with the education system of the time. Narayan had always loved writing and, in the early years, he earned a meagre income by contributing to some publications.

His first full-length novel, *Swami and Friends,* was rejected by a string of publishers. Then one of his friends, who was at Oxford, took the manuscript to writer Graham Greene, who recommended it to a publisher he knew. Finally, the novel was published and thus began Narayan's lasting friendship with Greene. *Swami and Friends* received good reviews but did not see huge sales. However, supported by Greene, Narayan got more of his works published.

Around the time of World War II, Narayan found it difficult to reach his English publishers. So he started his own publishing company. Indian Thoughts Publication turned out to be quite successful and still exists. By then, Narayan had built up a vast readership across the world and was also making enough money. He began to spend a lot of time travelling, apart from writing, and stayed active till his last days.

Narayan is probably best known for creating the fictional town of Malgudi, the semi-urban setting for most of his stories. It was first introduced in *Swami and Friends* and later found mention in several other narratives, gradually evolving with time. *Malgudi*

Days was also made into a popular televised serial on Doordarshan. Apart from fiction, he also wrote essays on varied topics; these were later collated in *The Writer's Nightmare* in 1987.

Narayan's iconic work *Guide* was made into a movie starring Dev Anand. Later, it was adapted for Broadway with the musical score by Ravi Shankar. *The Grandmother's Tale* (1992) was his last published work. His creative energies did not fade with time though, and he passed away while planning his next novel.

Narayan's style of writing has been compared to that of other acclaimed writers like O' Henry, Guy de Maupassant and Anton Chekhov. Although his language was simple, he infused his stories with wit, humour and irony, displaying deep insight into the minds of common people.

Narayan was nominated to the Rajya Sabha, where he served his six-year term. He received the Sahitya Akademi Award, the Padma Bhushan and the Padma Vibhushan. He was nominated for the Nobel Prize for Literature on many occasions. He is one of India's best known novelists.

The Storyteller

Name: Ruskin Bond
Birth Date: 19 May 1934
Place: Kasauli, Himachal Pradesh

Ruskin Bond has charmed us all with his easy smile and cheerful persona, which belie the unhappy experiences of his early childhood. Bond's parents separated when he was very young but he continued to share a close relationship with his father, who encouraged him to write and to keep a journal. Unfortunately, his father died of poor health when Bond was just ten years old.

After his father's death, Bond—who was at the time studying in a boarding school in Shimla—had to move to Dehradun to live with his grandmother. In later years, he spoke humorously of life with his grandmother who was a strict disciplinarian. Growing up in the hills exposed Bond to the beauty of nature. Simplicity and quaintness are reflected in his writings.

Bond wrote his first book, *The Room on the Roof*, when he was just seventeen and published it a few years later. Around this time, he also made up his mind to make a living as a writer. *The Room on the Roof* went on to win the John Llewellyn Rhys Memorial Prize in 1957. It was also adapted into a TV series by BBC. The sequel to this book was called *Vagrants in the Valley*.

Bond has said that writing is a part of him and he would most likely have continued to write even if his first book had not been published. Bond has written many stories, novels, poems and essays. He has not only been prolific but has also defied genres by writing on a variety of topics and attracting varied readers. His vast fan base comprises people of all age groups, and his literary exploits include everything from ghost stories to children's books to novels for adults.

Bond once spoke of how his first children's book happened more by chance than by design. He had written a story called 'The Angry River', which a publisher in England liked. However, the story was not long enough to be a novel for grown-ups, and was way too advanced to be read by children. The publisher suggested that Bond revise the story for a younger readership. Bond rewrote the story and that's how his first children's book happened.

Since then, many children across India and the world have grown up reading Bond's books, full of simple humour, wit, mischief, and the magic of nature. As he says, 'To be able to laugh and to be merciful are the only things that make man better than the beast.'

Bond continues to write even today. He also

continues to live in the hills, at Landour, Mussoorie, with his adopted family. Incidentally, Bond lived briefly in England in his younger years but, despite his British descent, England was not his cup of tea. He longed to be back in the hills and wilderness here, so he returned to India where he has lived ever since.

People who have had the opportunity of visiting his house speak of its simplicity. Much has also been said of the nature of Bond's innocent, uncomplicated existence despite his being one of the most widely read authors in the world.

Bond is a recipient of the Sahitya Akademi Award and the Padma Shri. His novel *A Flight of Pigeons* inspired *Junoon*, a cult film by Merchant-Ivory productions. *Scenes from a Writer's Life* and *A Lamp Is Lit* are his autobiographical works.

Silicon Valley
Entrepreneur

Name: Sabeer Bhatia
Birth Date: 30 December 1968
Place: Chandigarh

When he was just twenty-eight years old, this entrepreneur received one of the most important telephone calls of his life! He could not believe his ears when he was informed that the founder of Microsoft, Bill Gates, wanted to buy his company, which was just a year old then! When Bhatia entered the intimidating negotiations for the acquisition, he hardly knew that he would one day bask in glory, create history in the software industry and occupy one of the top slots among the ultra-rich entrepreneurs of Silicon Valley.

Initially, the panel of twelve negotiators from Microsoft offered to buy Hotmail, his free email web service, at a price of 160 million dollars. The confident young Bhatia had immense faith in his brainchild, the first of its kind, which already boasted of ten million subscribers within a year of being launched. He thought his brilliant idea was worth much more as Hotmail had welcomed its millionth customer within a few months after it caught the attention of web users. He followed his gut and negotiated wisely, having accurately assessed how interested his adversaries were in buying his idea. He shocked the Microsoft officials by refusing to close the deal for the amount they offered. His partners were truly worried.

A month later, Microsoft approached him again, this time with an offer of 350 million dollars. The deal was closed on 30 December 1997, Bhatia's twenty-ninth birthday, at a price of nearly three million Microsoft shares worth a whopping 400 million dollars then. Bhatia became a Silicon Valley legend, making business tycoons across the world sit up and notice.

During his graduation from BITS Pilani, Bhatia earned a full scholarship at California Institute of Technology, or CalTech. While pursuing his Masters at Stanford, Bhatia attended lectures by some inspirational legends, and resolved to achieve something that would make the world turn to him. When he started working at Apple Computers, he read about young dynamic entrepreneurs who had started business with a meagre capital, yet succeeded in selling millions of products to people with their innovative strategies.

Bhatia first developed Javasoft, a web-based database to store task lists, schedules, and albums online. After brainstorming with colleagues, he added email support that later brought about a huge transformation on the

Internet. Bhatia then came up with a business plan to launch this web-based email service. He initially found it really hard to find investors who were trying to grab the idea rather than invest in its potential. Finally, when Hotmail was launched on 4 July 1996, it became a rage among web users.

After the pricey acquisition by Microsoft, Bhatia went on to launch another revolutionary e-commerce venture named Arzoo; it failed during the dot-com burst. Later, Arzoo was relaunched as a travel portal. Bhatia's other notable ventures are InstaColl, Live Documents, and BlogEverywhere. Sabsebolo.com, a web conferencing facility, gained recognition among small and medium enterprises in the software market.

Bhatia has won many awards in his flourishing career. Apart from winning the Entrepreneur of the Year award in 1997 and the TR100 awarded by the Massachusetts Institute of Technology to young innovators, he was listed among 'People to Watch' by *Time* in 2002.

Bhatia married his long-time friend Tania Sharma in 2008. An MBA graduate, she is an entrepreneur herself. She started the online portal ayurveda.com in 2002 and served as the director of Goodcare Pharma.

Bhatia aspires to build a nano city in Haryana with high-rise commercial and residential buildings by collaborating with the state government. He has successfully proved that a simple business idea can create a whole transformation, irrespective of capital investment.

The Master Blaster

Name: Sachin Ramesh Tendulkar
Birth Date: 24 April 1973
Place: Bombay, Maharashtra

It was 1983. India had just won the World Cup under the brilliant captaincy of Kapil Dev. The triumph was instrumental in kindling interest in the flamboyant game of cricket in this ten-year-old boy. Motivated by his brother Ajit, he walked on to the field with a bat bigger than him and started playing the game. At that point, he had probably not even dreamt of charting the envious career graph that he finally did.

Coached by the reputed Ramakant Achrekar, he scored centuries in Ranji Trophy, Irani Trophy and Duleep Trophy and gained direct entry (bypassing the Under-19 league) into the international squad as the youngest Indian player. His dream had come true. He now shared the field with Kapil Dev, who had impressed him a few years ago with the historic win.

Sachin had been named by his father after the veteran music director Sachin Dev Burman. His father, Ramesh Tendulkar, was a teacher and a novelist and his mother,

Rajni, worked in the insurance sector. Though Ramesh Tendulkar was not a great cricket buff, he had full faith in Sachin's potential. In fact, when Sachin decided to choose cricket over studies, his parents completely supported his passion. Their unconditional trust went a long way in motivating Sachin during career highs and lows.

Surprisingly, this multitalented player was initially interested only in bowling. However, as his batting techniques improved he became a treat for spectators. He shattered numerous records in his illustrious journey. Having played on more than fifty grounds worldwide, including fast and bouncy tracks under adverse climatic conditions, Sachin has established himself as one of the greatest batsmen that India has ever produced.

Top-class bowlers dread his destructive innings as he attacks different kinds of deliveries with consummate ease. Tendulkar has been awarded Man of the Match and Man of the Series titles innumerable times. No wonder he is fondly called 'The Master Blaster'.

Sachin is a committed sportsman who plays for his country rather than for establishing personal records. He once displayed his patriotism by seeking permission to use the Indian flag emblem on his helmet. He also proved his sense of duty by winning a match for India just after completing his father's last rites in 1999.

Sachin's journey into the limelight has not been without challenges. He has suffered from a chronic back problem and also a tennis elbow that rendered him out of form briefly. He never lost hope though and made a strong comeback after recovering. His brief stint at captaincy was not very successful and he soon resigned. However, he never leaves any stone unturned when it comes to taking up challenges.

Despite the constant attention from media, critics, players and fans all over the world, Sachin has handled his fame with composure, poise and elegance. Though he has broken several records and created some of his own, Sachin likes to focus on the game and play passionately for the sheer love of cricket. As he says, 'I just keep it simple. Watch the ball and play it on merit.'

Sachin has always kept his personal life away from media glare. He married Anjali, a paediatrician, in 1995. The couple has two children, Sara and Arjun. Though Tendulkar often goes on long tours, the trust and bonding between the couple have strengthened over the years. Ironically, Anjali hardly enjoys watching a match when Sachin is playing as she becomes too tensed! She watches only the recordings later, when she is much more relaxed.

The master blaster is known for his philanthropic activities, such as sponsoring the education of many underprivileged children. However, he likes to keep his charitable initiatives away from media attention too.

This brilliant batsman is only 170 cm tall but has proved to the world that being short does not limit anyone from climbing higher. He is one of the highest paid and most popular cricketers of the world. He was the first to have scored fifty centuries in Test cricket and the first to score 10,000 runs in One-Day International (ODI) matches. He is also the first to have scored a double century in ODIs, in 2010 in Africa. He is the only Indian among the top ten in the ICC ranking released in February 2012. Recently, he crossed another milestone—he is now the first cricketer to have scored 100 centuries in international cricket.

It is no surprise that this cricketer has been conferred some of the most prestigious honours of the country— Padma Shri, Arjuna Award and Rajiv Gandhi Khel Ratna. He is a role model to many young cricketers who dream of making it big in the game.

The Queen of Badminton

Name: Saina Nehwal
Birth Date: 17 March 1990
Place: Hisar, Haryana

She has surprised world-class players with her splendid strokes and is currently the top ranked woman badminton player in India. Her striking consistency of performance earned her the title of 'Most Promising Player' in 2008 after she became the first Indian woman to win a Grand Prix title.

In the two stunning years that followed, Saina delivered her career's best performances. In 2008, she won the World Junior Badminton Championship. Her world ranking rose to number two as she enjoyed a hat-trick win at the Super Series tournaments. She was also the first woman to reach the singles quarterfinals at the Beijing Olympics in 2008. The proudest moment in her journey perhaps came when she won the gold medal at the Commonwealth Games 2010 held in India. In two consecutive years, 2011 and 2012, she won the gold at the Swiss Open Grand Prix.

Saina's battle was not restricted to the badminton court. She had quite a struggle before she finally stole the limelight and earned popularity. Born to former badminton champions Harvir Singh and Usha Nehwal, Saina received unconditional support from her parents in her childhood as the family together faced numerous challenges for nearly eight years, trying to guide their young daughter to where she is today.

It was coach Nani Prasad Rao who first noticed Saina's potential and asked Harvir to enrol her as a summer trainee. It was not an easy decision for a middle-class family to spend more than half its monthly income on the training, unsure of the consequences of the risk.

The challenging journey continued not only for young Saina but for her parents too. Her father would wake up every day at 4 a.m. and take her on his scooter to the stadium, twenty km away from their home. After a two-hour gruelling practice session, Saina was dropped to school, which was again another long journey. Travelling for nearly fifty km every day took a toll on her, making it tough for her to concentrate on her studies. Saina used to feel so exhausted that she would often fall asleep on her way to school. The family finally shifted home nearer to the stadium. Then Saina could attend practice sessions in the evenings too.

Soaring costs of training, transportation, and equipment in addition to skyrocketing telephone bills, especially during her international tours, made a dent in the savings of her parents. In fact, most of Saina's prize money was used to pay her mobile bills. Her lag on the educational front due to her constant tours was also a major concern for the family.

The financial struggle was relieved a little in 2002 when Saina received her sponsorship from Yonex. When she became the first Indian to win the Asian Satellite singles, she received financial support from Mittal Sports Trust. Also, Bharat Petroleum accepted her as an employee and took care of her travel expenditure. Surprisingly, the Sports Authority of India granted her extremely meagre funds nowhere near the actual requirements of a budding sports star.

Even after all this hard-earned glory, the family has not given in to exorbitant celebrations. They are content as Saina is now the proud recipient of the Arjuna Award and the coveted Rajiv Gandhi Khel Ratna. Saina is quite mature at handling success and is clearly focused on her sport and on improving her standing in the international circuit.

The badminton ace says, 'When I count what I have missed in life as a teenager and compare that with what I have achieved, I feel proud of my achievements. I am very happy with what I am doing now and I want to continue doing that.'

The Birdman of India

Name: Salim Ali
Birth Date: 12 November 1896
Place: Mumbai, British India
Death Date: 27 July 1987
Place: Bombay, Maharashtra

A ten-year-old boy once shot down a bird. He was curious about the yellow patch on the bird's neck. He wanted to know more about the species. He showed the bird to his uncle, a game hunter. When his uncle could not answer him, the boy took it to the Bombay Natural History Society and met its honorary secretary, W.S. Millard.

Millard was pleasantly surprised to find a young lad so inquisitive about birds. He brought out an exact model of the same bird and also introduced the boy to various other species, thus further kindling his interest. The young boy started visiting his office more often. This marked the beginning of Salim Moizuddin Abdul Ali's passion for birdwatching.

Salim's parents died when he was barely three. Along with his eight siblings, he then lived with his uncle.

Apart from his inclination for motorcycles and cricket, he was also interested in exploring the fascinating and colourful world of birds. He made birdcages from old crates or housed his feathered friends in cane baskets. Soon, he had a bird zoo in his backyard!

Salim was never really interested in mainstream studies and did not complete his graduation. He was called to work along with his brother in a mine in Burma but, even there, he was more engrossed in watching local birds. He returned to India to pursue a course in zoology and worked briefly as a museum guide at Bombay Natural History Society. He later went to Germany to learn about skinning and stuffing birds but, when he came back, he was out of a job due to funding problems at the museum.

Salim was married by then and began to work as a clerk to meet his financial needs. This left little time for him to pursue his real interest. He moved into a small house at Kihim, situated amidst trees and overlooking the harbour. In the monsoon, Salim got an opportunity to study the weaver birds that lived on the trees near his house. His observations about weaver birds and their nesting, mating and breeding habits were extraordinary. He patiently watched their activities for three to four months and came up with a publication in 1930 that won him acclaim in the field of ornithology.

Along with his supportive wife Tehmina, Salim travelled thousands of miles, exploring dangerous jungles, icy mountains and steep hills. He would walk about in heavy rubber shoes, carrying only a small pocket notebook and binoculars, spending the nights in leaky tents. It was quite a struggle to cover his expedition costs. During his journey as an ornithologist, he put in effort to protect and preserve many forests that would have otherwise been destroyed for personal use by nearby communities. He also worked towards setting up bird sanctuaries.

Salim documented several observations that conflicted with the theories of other reputed ornithologists. For instance, he discovered the Finn's Baya in the Kumaon hills, a bird that was believed to be extinct by then.

Salim realized that existing books on birds contained merely lengthy descriptions and were largely without any illustrations. Such books could not interest the common reader. In 1941, he brought out a book titled *The Book of Indian Birds* containing brief and interesting descriptions and colourful photographs to help people identify and become interested in various species.

In 1948, in collaboration with another reputed ornithologist S. Dillon Ripley, he started an ambitious project of bringing out nearly ten volumes of handbooks on the birds of Pakistan and India. The priceless editions not only highlighted the birds' appearances but also had details about their habits of migration and breeding. Salim is also credited with creating regional field guidebooks, such as those on the birds of Kerala, Sikkim and the Himalayas.

Salim Ali's works were recognized during his later years. He received many honours and awards, including the J. Paul Getty Wild Life Conservation Prize and the Padma Bhushan and Padma Vibhushan. The Netherlands honoured him with the Order of the Golden Ark. His inspirational work has gone a long way in giving recognition to the field of ornithology in India. He is rightly called 'The Birdman of India'.

Patriot and Poetess

Name: Sarojini Naidu
Birth Date: 13 February 1879
Place: Hyderabad, British India
Death Date: 2 March 1949
Place: Lucknow, Uttar Pradesh

> Weavers, weaving at break of day,
> Why do you weave a garment so gay?. . .
> Blue as the wing of a halcyon wild,
> We weave the robes of a new-born child.
>
> Weavers, weaving at fall of night,
> Why do you weave a garment so bright?. . .
> Like the plumes of a peacock, purple and green,
> We weave the marriage-veils of a queen.

This poem, 'Indian Weavers', is one of the gems in the collection titled *The Golden Threshold*. The poem describes the three important stages in human life—birth, marriage and death. The person who wrote this poem is none other than our 'Bharatiya Kokila', Sarojini Naidu. Her talents were not confined to poetry alone. She was also a renowned freedom fighter, an activist for women's rights and one of the greatest orators of her time.

Sarojini was born into a Brahmin family in Hyderabad. Her father, Aghoranath Chattopadhyay, was a noted scientist and philosopher. He founded Nizam College. Her mother, Barada Sundari Devi, was a Bengali poet. Sarojini was a brilliant student but she was not at all interested in the study of science and mathematics. Once, when she was eleven, she was trying to work out an algebra problem. She couldn't find the solution but a whole poem came to her suddenly and she jotted it down.

Her career as a poet began then. At thirteen, she wrote the 1,300-lines long *Lady of the Lake* in just six days. At the same age, she composed a 2,000-line play, which she had actually started writing just to spite her doctor, who had said that she was too ill to either read or write.

In one of her letters to Arthur Symons, noted poet and literary critic, she wrote: 'I am not a poet really. I have the vision and the desire, but not the voice. If I could write just one poem full of beauty and the spirit of greatness, I should be exultantly silent for ever; but I sing just as the birds do, and my songs are as ephemeral.'

Sarojini could use language effectively and persuasively, be it English or Persian. Her poetry is lyrical and musical. Her poems are filled with rich imagery and have the essence of Indian magic finding expression through a Western language. No wonder she is known as the Nightingale of India.

Her poetic works include *The Bird of Time: Songs of Life, Death & the Spring,* and *The Broken Wing: Songs of Love, Death and the Spring.* Two of her works, *The Sceptred Flute* and *The Feather of the Dawn,* were published posthumously. The latter was edited by her daughter, Padmaja Naidu.

Very early in life, Sarojini shot to fame when she topped the matriculation examination at the age of twelve. In 1895, Sarojini was sent to England with a special scholarship from the Nizam. She studied initially at King's College, London, and later at Girton College, Cambridge. In September 1898, Sarojini returned to Hyderabad and, breaking through the bonds of caste, married Govindarajulu Naidu, a non-Brahmin physician.

In the wake of the partition of Bengal in 1905, Sarojini joined the Indian national movement. She came into contact with great personalities like Gopal Krishna Gokhale, Rabindranath Tagore, Annie Besant, Jawaharlal Nehru, and Mahatma Gandhi. Gokhale advised her to rejuvenate the spirit of freedom in the hearts of villagers through her poetry.

In 1916, she met Gandhiji and immersed herself completely in the freedom movement. Thus began her role as a freedom fighter and orator. Apart from invoking nationalistic enthusiasm among Indians, she travelled across India to re-establish self-esteem in women and to encourage them to fight for their rights.

In 1925, Sarojini presided over the annual session of Indian National Congress at Kanpur. She was the first woman to hold the post of Congress president.

In 1928, she went to the US with the message of Gandhiji's non-violence movement. In 1930, after the Mahatma's arrest, she took on the helm of this movement. In 1931, she attended the Round Table Summit along with Gandhiji and Pandit Madan Mohan Malviya. During the Quit India movement, Sarojini was jailed for two years.

In 1947, she became the governor of Uttar Pradesh in free India. This too was a landmark achievement, as she was the first woman to serve as governor of an Indian state. Sarojini Naidu died in office, succumbing to a heart attack in March 1949.

India's Second President

Name: Sarvepalli Radhakrishnan
Birth Date: 5 September 1888
Place: Madras Presidency, British India
Death Date: 17 April 1975
Place: Madras, Tamil Nadu

A few people close to Dr Sarvepalli Radhakrishnan once wanted to celebrate his birthday, on 5 September. He told them that he would be happier if the day were celebrated as Teachers' Day rather than as his birthday alone.

Not a surprising response from a man who was himself a great teacher, apart from being a philosopher, an academician and a statesman. He appreciated the crucial role that teachers play in moulding young minds and influencing the nation's future. As per his wishes, 5 September is indeed celebrated as Teachers' Day in India.

Dr Radhakrishnan was born into a family of modest means and spent much of his early life in the temple town of Tirupati. He was thus exposed to many devotional activities. At the same time, he was also familiar with the theological activities at the Christian missionary school where he studied. Both influenced his thinking and shaped his philosophical perspective. He completed his masters in philosophy from the reputed Madras Christian College. What is remarkable about him is that he earned many scholarships in his academic life by virtue of his excellence in studies.

It is said that Dr Radhakrishnan first thought of pursuing philosophy when a relative after completing graduation handed over his old textbooks to him. While studying at Madras Christian College, Dr Radhakrishnan was introduced to European philosophy. Later, he started writing his own philosophical theories and thoughts. Many of his articles were published in international journals. He is credited with having opened up Indian philosophy to the West. He did a lot to make people of other cultures understand and appreciate the essence of Indian philosophy.

An Idealist View of Life is one of Dr Radhakrishnan's best known works. In this book, he tries to illustrate the importance of intuitive thinking as opposed to purely intellectual thought.

Dr Radhakrishnan was a great admirer of Swami Vivekananda and Rabindranath Tagore. He espoused a form of Hinduism called Vedanta, which he believed focused on finding personal spiritual meaning and growth.

During his academic career, Dr Radhakrishnan held many distinguished offices such as the prestigious George V Chair of Mental and Moral Science at University of Calcutta. He was invited to deliver lectures at Harris Manchester College, Oxford. He also served as vice chancellor of Andhra University before the University of Oxford appointed him to the H.N. Spalding Chair of Eastern Religions and Ethics. Later, back in India, he worked as vice chancellor of Benaras Hindu University.

After India gained independence, Dr Radhakrishnan became actively involved in the nation's political activities. He served as a member of the Constituent Assembly. Prime Minister Jawaharlal Nehru appointed him India's ambassador to Moscow. His political growth continued as he soon became a Rajya Sabha member. He served as vice-president of India for several years before becoming the country's second president in 1962.

In 1989, the University of Oxford instituted the Radhakrishnan Scholarships in the name of this great scholar. These later came to be known as the Radhakrishnan Chevening Scholarships. He was nominated four times for the Nobel Prize in Literature. Dr Radhakrishnan is also a recipient of the Bharat Ratna.

Rocket Scientist

Name: Satish Dhawan
Birth Date: 25 September 1920
Place: Srinagar, Kashmir
Death Date: 3 March 2002
Place: Bangalore, Karnataka

It was 1979. It was one of the most exciting times for the Indian Space Research Organization (ISRO) as India's satellite launch vehicle, SLV-3, was to be launched to put the satellite Rohini into its orbit. Dr A.P.J. Abdul Kalam was its project director. Thousands of people had spent sleepless nights to achieve this mission.

A few minutes before the launch, the computer program that ran the checklist indicated a few warnings. It suggested that the launch should be put on hold as some components were not functioning as expected.

The experts assured Dr Kalam that they had repeatedly checked the functioning of the components and that the result would be in their favour. Finally, the team decided to ignore the warning reports and proceed with the launch. Unfortunately, the mission

ended in a tragic failure. All the hard work put in by
the scientists disintegrated deep down into the Bay of
Bengal.

It was a crucial time at ISRO. A press conference was
scheduled just after the launch. Journalists from around
the world had gathered to witness the event. The ISRO
chairman decided to accept responsibility and held the
press conference himself. He told the media that the
team had worked very hard though the mission had
failed. The project would be launched again within a
year, with additional technological support.

True to his words, the following year, in July 1980,
the satellite was launched successfully. ISRO made
India proud and the nation was jubilant. This time
around, the chairman congratulated Dr Kalam and
asked him to hold the press conference. Dr Kalam
later mentioned that it was a day of true revelation for
him. When the team had failed, this exemplary leader
bravely acknowledged the responsibility, but when the
team succeeded, he let them enjoy the laurels.

The ISRO chairman, who handled the failure and
churned out success with such brilliance, was Prof.
Satish Dhawan, the outstanding scientist who shaped the
Indian space programme and proved with his conviction
that his countrymen have the potential to develop
self-sufficiency and expertise in space technology. He
explored the potential of using science and technology
for various socially constructive purposes that could
impact the nation as a whole. He was an encouraging

teacher and an institution builder. He also holds the credit of being one of the longest serving directors of the Indian Institute of Science (IISc).

Prof. Dhawan was born in Kashmir, completed his Bachelors and Masters from the University of Punjab and went abroad to pursue higher studies in aeronautical engineering at Caltech. He started his career at IISc as a senior scientific officer and was noticed for his brilliance and zest. Very soon, he went on to teach there and became head of the department within four years of joining. When he was just forty-two years old, he became the youngest director of IISc. During his successful tenure, he identified bright and motivated faculty from India and abroad and brought them together at the institute to promote the spirit of research in relatively new and unexplored areas.

Prof. Dhawan took over the space programme after Vikram Sarabhai, who had envisioned developing satellites for beneficial applications like direct TV broadcasting, meteorological research and remote sensing. Prof. Dhawan formed the organization structure and set up the required processes to promote systematic research and development. He believed in collective decision-making strategies that would help monitor progress. His methods were built on coordination across organizations and focus groups within ISRO, while involving other industries and premier academic institutions.

Prof. Dhawan always thought of himself as an

academician first, then a scientist. Hence, he continued to serve as a director of IISc while serving ISRO. He came up with methods to develop and launch satellites on stringent budgets. Before this, satellite launching projects had created national euphoria. Under his leadership, satellite technology was built in India by Indians within the same bureaucratic set-up that many loved to criticize.

If the Indian space programme has become mature and flaunts spectacular growth, the credit goes to this visionary who always kept in mind the social implications of the advances. His confidence in the potential of Indian engineers was so phenomenal that he protected them from the blame of peers when their honest attempts failed.

Prof. Dhawan is the recipient of several honours and awards, notably Padma Vibhushan and Indira Gandhi Award for National Integration. In recognition of his outstanding contributions, the Indian satellite launch centre at Sriharikota, Andhra Pradesh, has been renamed as the Satish Dhawan Space Centre.

Silver Screen Giant

Name: Satyajit Ray
Birth Date: 2 May 1921
Place: Calcutta, Bengal, British India
Death Date: 23 April 1992
Place: Calcutta, West Bengal

His grandfather founded a printing press in 1895 and started *Sandesh*, the hugely popular Bengali magazine for young people, in 1913. His father wrote amazing poems containing simple humour, which delight readers to this day. His family embraced Brahmo Samaj, a sect within Hindu society, in 1880.

This stalwart is one of the greatest Indian film-makers to have left behind the legacy of a cinematic heritage that belongs not only to India but to the whole world.

Yes, he is none other than Satyajit Ray. Born to Sukumar and Suprabha Ray, he was much adored as a child, which earned him his pet name Manik ('jewel'). He grew up in an extended family of cousins and was exposed to both Eastern and Western cultures. He was schooled in Calcutta and graduated in economics from Presidency College. In 1940, he joined Visva-Bharati University in Santiniketan to study art under the guidance of Nandalal Bose and Binode Behari Mukherjee.

As a child, Ray developed two significant interests, which he later integrated into his work. One was his passion for cinema and the other was his deep interest in Western classical music. As a young man, he read books on film-making and wrote screenplays to amuse himself.

Ray joined the British advertising agency D.J. Keymer in 1943 as a junior designer and there he learnt the art of book-jacket designing, graphic art, typography and illustration. Later, he was sent to London on work by the company. This gave Ray the opportunity of his lifetime as he saw many films like Vittorio De Sica's *Ladri di Biciclette* ('Bicycle Thieves') and Jean Renoir's *La Règle du Jeu* ('Rules of the Game'), which made a lasting impression on him.

On returning from London, Ray worked for a publishing house and set up a film society in cooperation with others. At this time, he also illustrated a book called *Pather Panchali* written by Bibhuti Bhushan Bandopadhyaya. There and then, he decided to create a film out of the novel. Despite financial and production obstacles, he managed to complete and release *Pather Panchali* in 1955. This film brought him instant national and international acclaim. His path was chalked out. He became a full-time film-maker and went on to make twenty-seven feature films and a few documentaries and short films, too.

Ray's films did not only have a regional appeal but were well received both nationally and internationally. Portraying universal emotions and human relationships, they reached out across myriad genres of cinema-goers in the world.

It is believed that the progressive outlook of the Brahmo Samaj strongly influenced Ray's work. Many of his films including *Devi, Charulata, Teen Kanya, Sadgati, Ghare Baire,* and *Ganashatru* give us a glimpse of his strong aversion to religious fanaticism. They also reveal the strong influence of Tagore. Ray's cinematic productions include musical fantasies like *Goopy Gayen Bagha Bayen,* detective fiction like *Sonar Kella,* and historical drama like *Shatranj ke Khiladi.*

Ray received several national and international awards. The Padma Shri, Padma Bhushan, Padma Vibhushan and Bharat Ratna were conferred on him by the Government of India. Ray was the second film personality after Charles Chaplin to have been awarded an honorary doctorate by the University of Oxford. He also received the Legion of Honour from the French government in 1987, while the Academy Award for Lifetime Achievement was awarded to him in 1992.

Paying rich tribute to Ray, acclaimed film-maker Akira Kurosawa said, 'The quiet but deep observation, understanding and love of the human race, which are characteristic of all his films, have impressed me greatly. ...I feel that he (Ray) is a "giant" of the movie industry... Not to have seen the cinema of Ray means existing in the world without seeing the sun or the moon.'

Though film-making was his first love, Ray had a passion for writing as well. He revived his grandfather's magazine *Sandesh*, writing and illustrating the stories himself. At the behest of the editor of a popular Bengali magazine, *Desh*, Ray wrote a short novel for its annual edition. This was the beginning of his literary career. Then on, he penned several short stories and their translations. All of them became bestsellers in Bengal and some of them were later filmed.

In 1983, Satyajit Ray suffered a massive heart attack. He remained an acute heart patient from then on till his death in 1992. However, in the interim, he did continue working and produced films like *Ghare Baire* (1984), *Ganashatru* (1989) and *Agantuk* (1992).

Ray's works live on. His brilliant cinematic productions as well as his fiction—fantasy, suspense, science fiction—continue to charm both children and adults.

Baadshah of Bollywood

Name: Shah Rukh Khan
Birth Date: 2 November 1965
Place: New Delhi

When he first appeared in the TV series *Fauji* in 1988, Col Kapoor, who had been instrumental in casting him, was impressed with his zest and enthusiasm. The dynamic young boy had such spark that he could not sit idle for even a moment. Col Kapoor predicted that this bubbly young man would go places in his profession. It is unlikely, though, that even he could have envisaged Shah Rukh's astounding rise to superstardom.

After working in another TV series called *Circus*, followed by a small role in an English film made for TV and written by Arundhati Roy, Shah Rukh got his first chance in a Hindi movie.

Hema Malini, the 'Dream Girl' of Bollywood, was apprehensive about casting him in her directorial debut in 1991, *Dil Aashna Hai*. His unconventional looks,

average height, flamboyant hair, and big nose were
major causes of concern. When the film bombed at
the box office, little did one expect that this youngster
would later reign over the Hindi film industry, giving
his contemporaries quite a run for their money.

Shah Rukh Khan hails from a non-film family. His
father was an Independence activist. The family lived
in Delhi where Shah Rukh did his schooling. He was
an all-rounder at school and loved sports. In fact,
he believes that sports should be an integral part of
education. Later he graduated in economics from
University of Delhi.

The journey of this boy-next-door to superstardom
was not without its share of struggles. It was a feat
in itself as he had no backing from film veterans.
His simple nature and his never-say-die attitude took
him a long way to reach the position of a superstar
in constant limelight. Shah Rukh lost his parents at a
young age. He shifted to Mumbai and married Gauri
even before he had established himself as a leading
actor. His supportive wife stood by him like a rock and
encouraged him. Shah Rukh is widely appreciated as
a thorough family man and a doting father to his two
children, Aryan and Suhana. How does he balance his
professional and personal life? Well, he has a naughty
twinkle in his eyes as he quips: 'Whenever I fail as a
father or husband, a toy and a diamond always work.'

After his smashing debut in *Deewana*, for which he
won the Filmfare Award, the audience, expected a whole

new world of entertainment out of him. Indeed, in a very short time, he charmed people with his charismatic nature and captivated their attention. He has acted in a wide variety of genres such as romances, thrillers, historical drama, sports films and comedies. The fact that he breathes dreams and lives films is evident in his own words: 'Cinema in India is like brushing your teeth in the morning. You can't escape it.'

As a man of integrity, he also respects all religions alike and celebrates all major Indian festivals at his residence with fervour.

Exhaustion is not known to Shah Rukh. Everyone admires him for his wit and humour. Not surprisingly, with his contagious energy and a rare sense of humour, he has made valuable friends and enjoyed long associations with top production banners. His willingness to constantly improve in his craft and his professionalism have taken him to where he is today.

Shah Rukh started Dreamz Unlimited, a production house, with his long-time friend Juhi Chawla as a partner. His initial ventures such as *Phir Bhi Dil Hai Hindustani* as a producer bombed but he continued delivering major blockbusters like *Main Hoon Na* and *Om Shanti Om* in his acting career and retained his envious position. Shah Rukh also owns Red Chillies Entertainment and sponsors the Kolkata Knight Riders team in the Indian Premier League. The team has just won IPL 2012.

Shah Rukh has enjoyed a successful stint in television.

Apart from endorsing leading brands, he established his versatility as a TV presenter by hosting shows like *Kaun Banega Crorepati* and *Kya Aap Paanchvi Pass Se Tez Hain*? Shah Rukh never hesitates to perform at social functions as he believes in entertainment in all mediums.

The King of Bollywood, fondly called SRK in the industry, has acted in over seventy films. For his exemplary work in Indian cinema, SRK has bagged fourteen Filmfare awards and is also the actor with the highest number of awards in the Best Actor category. In recognition of his achievements, SRK has been conferred the Padma Shri. Three of his wax statues have been unveiled in Europe, two at Madame Tussauds in London, and the third at Musée Grévin in Paris.

The Human Calculator

Name: Shakuntala Devi
Birth Date: 4 November 1939
Place: Bangalore, Karnataka

It was 18 June 1980. The computer department of Imperial College in London had randomly picked two thirteen-digit numbers: 7,686,369,774,870 and 2,465,099,745,770. These were to be multiplied. An Indian lady answered the question in just twenty-eight seconds. Something that had been a natural talent to her for years came as an astonishing revelation to the world. Her correct answer—18,947,668,177,995,42 6,462,773,730—won her a mention in the *Guinness Book of World Records*.

She had earlier extracted the 23rd root of a 201 digit number mentally in 1977. Calculating prodigy Shakuntala Devi is India's pride.

She was born into a Brahmin family in Bangalore, Karnataka. Her father worked in a circus as a trapeze and tightrope performer, and later as a lion tamer and a human cannonball. In her humble surroundings, Shakuntala demonstrated extraordinary calculation skills at a very early age. Once, when she was playing cards with her father at the age of three, she beat him in the game not by sleight of the hand but by memorizing the cards.

Shakuntala received her early training in mathematics from her grandfather. At five years of age, she demonstrated the ability to solve complex arithmetic mentally. At six, she demonstrated her calculation and memorization abilities to a large audience at the University of Mysore and repeated a similar achievement at the age of eight at Annamalai University.

Many calculating prodigies across the world have been known to lose their gift over the years. However, Shakuntala Devi continues to solve complicated mathematical problems with lightning rapidity and precision. She encourages young children to explore and discover the world of mathematics. She believes that a child's ability to learn is exceptional and that given correct nurturing, each child will be able to develop inborn strengths. To promote this ability in children, Shakuntala Devi organizes workshops and publishes books. Her book, *Wonderland of Numbers*, speaks of a young girl called Neha and her love for numerals.

Shakuntala Devi travels across the world to perform and inspire people. She has used her unique ability with numbers and combined it with astrology to make predictions. Her clients include many well known personalities and celebrities. Apart from books, puzzles and mathematics contests for children, she has also authored books on astrology. Her passionate interest in her subjects led her to develop the concept of 'mind dynamics' which believes in exploring and developing the learning power of the human mind.

In 1950, still quite young, Shakuntala sailed to Europe. In London on 5 October 1950, the British Broadcasting Corporation presented Shakuntala to the viewers of Great Britain. Shakuntala gave quick answers to problems posed by the BBC but when further questions were given, she challenged the problems as being incorrect. Leslie Mitchell, the interviewer, did some quick checking and confessed that Shakuntala was indeed right and the BBC wrong.

Despite her unique abilities, Shakuntala Devi dislikes the credit and title of 'human computer' that is often used to describe her. She strongly believes that human minds have a much larger potential and can perform better than any computer.

Some of her books are *Puzzles To Puzzle You, Book of Numbers, Figuring: The Joy of Numbers In the Wonderland of Numbers,* and *Mathability: Awaken the Math Genius in Your Child.*

Shakuntala Devi is a living example of how natural talent, if nurtured well, can conquer the world. Her life inspires every parent to believe in their child's innate abilities.

Spiritual Scholar and Teacher

Name: Shankaracharya
Birth Date: AD 788
Place: Kaladi, Kerala
Death Date: AD 820
Place: Kedarnath, now in Uttarakhand

Shankaracharya was once on a journey with his disciples. They came across a person from a lower caste. Although Shankaracharya was then already an established spiritual scholar and teacher, he still believed in the system of untouchability. He and his disciples asked the lower-caste man to step aside so that they could pass by without making contact with him. At this, the man asked them a question. He said that his body too was made of flesh and blood and performed the same functions as theirs; his soul too was unconnected with the physical aspects of the body just like theirs; so which of these was untouchable? Did they want his body to step aside or his soul?

This question awakened Shankaracharya to his own error of understanding. It prompted him to write five verses known as *Manisha Panchakas*. The theme of these verses is that man can only claim to be enlightened if he can see the world and all its beings as a part of himself, without discriminating one from the other as high or low; and a man who can do this can be considered a guru or teacher, irrespective of the community or caste into which he is born.

Shankaracharya is famous today for propagating the philosophy of *advaita* or non-dualism. According to this complex philosophy, there is only one truth or reality. The universe and all its beings do not exist by themselves but are part of one supreme, eternal reality.

Born in Kerala, Shankaracharya was a prodigious child who is said to have mastered all the four Vedas by the time he was eight. He was fluent not just in his mother tongue Malayalam but also in Sanskrit. At a very young age, he made up his mind to renounce family and material pursuits and devote his life to spiritual learning. Although his mother was not very happy with his decision, she finally accepted it.

Shankaracharya went around looking for a guru who could lead him towards enlightenment. He finally found his teacher in a man called Govinda Bhagvatpada. At their first meeting itself, the guru is said to have been impressed by Shankaracharya's understanding of the concept of non-dualism. After a period of intense study, Shankaracharya travelled across India to share his learning with others. He promoted the Vedantic principle that Brahman (the Supreme) and man are of one essence and that people should try to cultivate this vision of oneness. He participated in debates with other spiritual leaders where he compared Advaita with other schools of thought. He also set up four institutions called *mathas* to propagate his philosophy, and placed his four main disciples in charge of one *matha* each. Located in Sringeri (Karnataka), Dwarka (Gujarat), Puri (Orissa) and Joshi (Uttarakhand), these four *mathas* are still extant.

Shankaracharya wrote many commentaries on ancient texts like the Upanishads and the Bhagavad Gita. *Bhaja Govindam*, a book of devotional poems in Sanskrit, is another of his noted works.

Although Shankaracharya is said to have lived for a very short period of around thirty years, he led an active life teaching and writing about his spiritual philosophy right till the end. His intellectual and spiritual powers continue to impress us to this very day.

Superstar of the South

Name: Shivaji Rao Gaekwad
Birth Date: 12 December 1949
Place: Bangalore, Karnataka

Shivaji Rao Gaekwad was born into a Maharashtrian family. He lost his mother when he was just five. With three siblings to support, he was compelled to take up odd jobs to cater to the basic needs of his family while striving to continue his education. After a difficult childhood, he became a conductor in the government bus service at Bangalore. There he met Raja Bahadur, a driver.

Shivaji and Raja became good friends and enjoyed watching movies in local theatres. Shivaji used to act in stage plays and Raja noticed his potential to captivate the audience. This selfless friend advised his buddy to aim higher in life and suggested that he should try his hand at acting in films. He convinced young Shivaji to enrol at the Adyar Film Institute in Chennai.

Shivaji was reluctant to give up his government job due to financial responsibilities but Raja promised to support Shivaji for the two years that he trained at the film institute. He kept his word by giving a significant part of his salary to his friend until he completed the course.

Finally, after the course, Shivaji got a break when the famous director Balachander noticed a spark in him and signed him up for a role in a Tamil movie. Since another famous movie star named Sivaji was already reigning over the industry then, Balachander gave Shivaji Gaekwad a new screen name.

The first role for this actor seemed inauspicious. He played a terminally ill patient, dressed in rags, opening a gate while smoking a *beedi*. He was on screen for barely fifteen minutes. The movie, *Aboorva Ragangal*, which went on to win a National Award, was released amid much controversy. The audience never thought that this debutant would later win millions of hearts all over the world and command undisputable stardom for decades to come. The director Balachander was sure though that this actor would take all of Tamil Nadu by storm. The actor, who still considers him his guru, went on to prove his judgement true.

With a string of anti-hero roles and a refreshing acting style, this new wonder of the film industry captured the attention of every producer who wanted optimum return on investment. Today, almost every actor craves to be like him and every new actress dreams of being a part of the movie in which he is acting. All of us know him today by one of the most influential names of Tamil cinema—Rajnikanth. And his punchlines have become the stuff of legends.

Rajni's humble beginning was no hurdle as he enthralled audiences with his versatility and powerful screen presence in numerous films like *Bhairavi*, *Thalapathi* and *Netrikan*. He catapulted to stardom at an unimaginable pace.

People flocked to the theatres just to see him. There was thunderous applause for his stunts as well as his comic timing. With roles as diverse as an abusive husband, a village rowdy, a failed lover, and a Hindu saint he was soon the reigning superstar within a few years of stepping into the industry. He proved as capable of experimentation as of versatility. He has played triple roles and worked in multilingual productions. *Raja Chinna Roja* was the first Indian film to use animated characters along with human actors.

Surprisingly, he found it quite stressful to handle the sudden media glare, popularity and money. He wanted to quit at the peak of his career! This shocked all his fans. His well-wishers asked him to stay on. After that, there was no going back. Rajni has not only created waves among Tamil audiences but also has a huge global fan following. Some of his movies like *Muthu* were dubbed into Japanese and ran successfully. He has also worked in Hindi movies like *Andhaa Kanoon* and *Hum*, in Bengali films like *Bhagya Devata*, in Malayalam films like *Dharma Yuddam*, and even an English film called *Bloodstone*.

Despite having suffered several health challenges, Rajni is still considered a superstar and yet is one of the most affable actors around. He is a strong believer in spirituality. He also wields strong political influence. He is deeply committed to social issues and has campaigned against civil war in Sri Lanka. He remains grounded in reality and never fails to keep in touch with his beloved friend who made this entire transformation possible.

Raja Bahadur remains the first and perhaps the greatest fan of Rajnikanth and still fondly refers to him as Shivaji. He never misses out on watching a Rajni movie, first day, first show!

The Kathak Queen

Name: Shovana Narayan
Birth Date: 2 November, 1950
Place: Calcutta, West Bengal

This legendary Kathak performer believes that dance is the medium to discover the rare blend of spirituality, truth and beauty. Her ghungroos respond effortlessly to her innovative and spellbinding choreography. Her elegant movements, her expressive eyes and her graceful footwork have established her as an eminent dancer during her flourishing journey of four decades.

Shovana began learning Kathak at the tender age of four, initially under the mentorship of Sadhana Bose followed by Guru Kundanlal. As one of the first disciples of the acclaimed Kathak maestro Birju Maharaj, she developed her remarkable talent and amalgamated the Western and Indian art forms giving them wider dimension in her experimental fusion works. Shovana has mesmerized audiences with her mind-blowing multiple roles in a single performance.

A personification of sensitivity and grace, Shovana has collaborated successfully with renowned musicians, ballet troupes and tap dancers, thus breaking both linguistic and regional barriers. In her performance titled *Moonlight Impressionism*, she swayed to music composed by stalwarts like Beethoven, Ravel and Mozart. *The Dawn After* saw her blend classical Indian dance with Spanish flamenco and Western classical ballet. Her outstanding performances at national and international art festivals have won her global recognition.

Shovana was one of the first dancers to draw inspiration from the lives of legends like Ramana Maharshi, Vivekananda, Mahatma Gandhi and Ramkrishna Paramhamsa and touch upon various philosophical themes and socially sensitive issues in her versatile portrayal of roles. Through *Shakuntala*, she rejuvenated the North Indian narrative dance form called soliloquy. Her operatic performances like *Wicchare Pani* and *Ghalib ki Dilli* gained instant appreciation among audiences.

A staunch believer of the gurukul parampara, Shovana Narayan goes to great lengths to identify the strengths and the stylistic individuality in her students. She has imparted her knowledge of Kathak to emerging performers and successfully cultivated many acclaimed dancers at the Asavari Centre of Dance. Her dance troupe is known for its revolutionary thematic ideas and innovative explorations of social issues through rhythm.

The danseuse organizes two popular art festivals annually. One invites famous dance maestros to perform on stage; the other showcases the talents of budding artists. This zestful visionary has authored ten books on dance traditions and other performing arts of India. She conceived and executed the opening and closing ceremonies of the 2010 Commonwealth Games held in Delhi.

Shovana's dynamic and individualistic approach to life has helped her successfully balance her dual professional responsibilities as a danseuse and a senior civil servant. She is married to Dr Herbert Traxi who has served as Austria's ambassador to India. Most artists of her stature would, perhaps, retire from academics but Shovana has recently completed a double MPhil from Madras and Punjab universities.

The Kathak Queen has received prestigious honours like the Padma Shri and Sangeet Natak Akademi Award in addition to the Rajiv Gandhi Puraskar and Bihar Gaurav Puraskar. She has etched out an inspirational life story through her professional achievements and her socially responsible activities, and is a role model for many young artists today.

Pioneer of New Cinema

Name: Shyam Benegal
Birth Date: 14 December 1934
Place: Trimulgherry, Hyderabad

When Shyam was just twelve years old, he made a short film using a handheld camera gifted to him by his father, a still photographer. Shyam's fascination with films persisted through his college years. He founded a film society while pursuing his studies at Osmania University.

However, Shyam Benegal started his professional career not as a moviemaker but as an advertising copywriter in Bombay. It was not long before he was promoted to a senior position where he had to write scripts and direct advertising films. He also made documentaries around this time, and taught for a period at the Film and Television Institute of India. His first feature film happened much later, when he was forty.

Benegal's debut film was *Ankur*. Its story revolved around the exploitation of the poor working class people by their rich employers. The film shot to fame and went on to win National Film Awards for both Benegal and lead actress Shabana Azmi.

After *Ankur*, Benegal continued to focus on social issues, women's rights, the search for identity, and other themes considered unconventional then. *Nishant, Manthan* and *Bhumika*, his next three films, brought him much acclaim. His movies came to be regarded as alternative or parallel cinema—distinct from the mainstream cinema that audiences were used to.

Remarkably, despite using quite unconventional themes, many of his movies received not only critical appreciation but also commercial success. They bridged the gap between the two extremes—'art films' that didn't make any money and 'masala films' that lacked quality and aesthetic value.

Interestingly, in a few cases, the financiers of Benegal's movies turned out to be as unconventional as the movies. There is a remarkable story behind the financing of *Manthan*. Its plot revolves around a set of poor farmers who break free of exploitation and find prosperity by forming a cooperative union. The movie was inspired by—and also financed by—the five lakh farmers who were members of the Gujarat Cooperative Milk Marketing Federation Ltd. Each of them donated two rupees to fund the film, which held much resemblance to the events of the lives. When it was released, they came in truckloads to see 'their film'. Not surprisingly, *Manthan* set the box office on fire.

Over the years, Benegal also made a number of movies that were biographical or historical, such as *Junoon, Satyajit Ray the Film-maker, Netaji Subhash Chandra Bose: The Forgotten Hero*, and *Sardari Begum*, among others. During the 1980s, he directed the widely watched TV serial *Bharat Ek Khoj*, based on Jawaharlal Nehru's book *Discovery of India*. Through his films, Benegal is credited with having brought into the limelight many actors of very high calibre such as Shabana Azmi, Naseeruddin Shah, Smita Patil and Om Puri.

Benegal is a recipient of the Padma Shri, the Padma Bhushan and the Dada Saheb Phalke Award. He has also won the National Award for Best Feature Film on seven occasions. Currently, he is engaged in directing an epic musical as well as a historical drama.

Performer Extraordinaire

Name: Sonal Mansingh
Birth Date: 30 April 1944
Place: Bombay Province, British India

I found love in Georg. Georg Lechner, the then director of Max Muller Bhavan. Georg offered me support when I needed it the most; we got engaged.

An accident changed my life. On 24 August 1974, Georg and I were driving down a wet, lonely highway in Germany when our car met with an accident. X-rays showed that my 12th vertebra was injured. I lost all reflexes in my toes, knees, ankles and elbows. I asked myself why I should stay alive when I couldn't dance again. Then, chiropractor Pierre Gravel came into my life.

Gravel gave me a new lease of life. After studying my reports and observing my condition for a few days, Gravel said, "I'm afraid... that you may be able to dance again!" From then on, I put all my energies into recovering. I came back to India within 11 months. On May 4, 1975, I performed to thunderous applause from a huge crowd.

I am always open to love. After being married for long, Georg and I parted ways. But love never went out of my life. I am always open to love.

[Sonal Mansingh: The dance of life, The *Times of India*]

This is the story of a danseuse, who suffered two failed marriages and a serious car accident but did not let the setbacks of life deter her. Her indomitable will made her relentlessly pursue her goal—the goal of using her art as an instrument of social change. This is the story of Sonal Mansingh.

Sonal was born into a Gujarati family in Mumbai. Her mother, Poornima Pakwasa, was a pious lady with a love for creative art. Her father, Arvind Pakwasa, was a prominent social worker. Her grandfather, Mangal Das Pakwasa, was a freedom fighter and one of the first five governors of India.

Sonal is one of India's finest classical dancers and has made her mark in the Odissi style of dance. She started learning Manipuri dance at the age of four. At seven, she moved on to learning Bharatanatyam from various gurus of the Pandanallur School. But her real training in dance began at the age of eighteen when, despite protests from her family, she went to Bangalore to learn Bharatanatyam from Prof. U.S. Krishna Rao and Chandrabhaga Devi. After her *arangetram* in Bombay, however, she chose to master Odissi under Guru Kelucharan Mohapatra.

In 1977, she founded the Delhi-based Centre for Indian Classical Dances, which has produced numerous stage productions and nurtured many notable artists. Her choreographies include *Indradhanush, Manavatta, Draupadi, Mera Bharat, Gita Govinda, Panchkanya, Chaturang, Devi Durga, Aatmayan,* and *Samanavaya.*

Jiwan Pani, a leading Oriya poet-lyricist and distinguished scholar of the performing arts, had been associated from the beginning with the institution the beginning and has guided Sonal in all her dance presentations from 1974 onwards. With his unflagging help, Sonal was able to build up a completely authentic and new repertoire of Odissi dance.

Although she is best known for Odissi, Sonal Mansingh is also an exponent of Bharatanatyam, Kuchipudi and Chhau. She is recognized the world over for her skills as a social reformer, philosopher, orator, choreographer, and trainer. Her work often deals with issues concerning women, environment and prison reforms.

Her achievements are many. She was the first dancer to bring Odissi to South India—Bharatanatyam has always been the main dance form there—as far back as 1969. She is an elected member of the executive board and general council of the Sangeet Natak Akademi. She has also been appointed a trustee of the largest institution for arts in India, the Indira Gandhi National Centre for the Arts.

Sonal Mansingh's exceptional talent has brought her many honours and awards, including Medals of

Friendship of Vietnam and Cuba State Council, Natya Kala Ratna from National Cultural Organization and the Sangeet Natak Akademi Award. In 1992, she became the youngest recipient of the Padma Bhushan. In 2003, she became the first female dancer to be awarded the Padma Vibhushan.

Sonal Mansingh believes that a lot of sacrifice and hard work goes into the arduous journey of becoming a dancer. According to her, one should interpret dance as a form of *sadhana*. It should be a commitment for life. She says, 'I am convinced that dance is the ultimate yoga in which body, mind and soul harmonize to create an experience of bliss which is *ananda*, the perfect state of being.'

Netaji

Name: Subhas Chandra Bose
Birth Date: 23 January 1897
Place: Cuttack, Orissa
Death Date: 18 August 1945 (not verified)

He believed that the path to freedom was to be paved with the blood of martyrs. He said, 'To my countrymen I say forget not that the grossest crime is to compromise with injustice and wrong.'

Who was this firebrand? He was Subhas Chandra Bose, the revolutionary freedom fighter of the Indian independence movement, known to us all as Netaji. He believed that British colonial rule could be ended only through forcible resistance.

Subhas was born into the family of Janakinath Bose, a rich and successful lawyer in Cuttack, ordained as 'Rai Bahadur'. His mother, Prabhavati Devi, was a religious lady and a follower of Ramakrishna Paramhamsa. She inculcated spiritual values in her children and this may have been one of the reasons that Subhas was deeply influenced by Swami Vivekananda.

Subhas was schooled in a Protestant European School in Calcutta. He was an intelligent student and stood second in his matriculation examination. He went on to study philosophy at Presidency College, Calcutta. In college, he developed political and social awareness. He noted how the British insulted Indians in public places. His nationalistic tendencies came to light when he and some of his friends were expelled from college for assaulting Professor Oaten, who had voiced anti-India comments and also manhandled some Indian students.

Janakinath wanted Subhas to become a civil servant, so he sent him to England for the Indian Civil Services examination. Subhas scored very well and qualified for automatic appointment but then he took his first conscious step as a revolutionary by refusing this employment. 'The best way to end a government is to withdraw from it,' he believed.

Subhas Chandra Bose returned to India in 1921. Back home, he joined the Indian National Congress led by Mahatma Gandhi, whom he was to later address in a radio talk in 1944 for the first time as 'Father of the Nation'. Although both differed in their ideologies, the two patriots respected each other. They shared another common quality—unwavering faith in God. Subhas always kept a pocket edition of the Bhagavad Gita under his pillow. He truly followed in the ethic and philosophy of the Gita. He believed, 'How can I possibly accept ahimsa as an inflexible principle of action, when Krishna himself exhorted Arjuna not to run away from a righteous war, a *dharmayuddha*?'

Subhas Bose and a few other leaders wanted 'complete self-rule, without any compromise' whereas Gandhi and other senior leaders favoured 'dominion status' for India within British rule. Differences grew and Subhas resigned from the party to form the Forward Bloc in 1939. He initiated a mass movement and received tremendous response from people across India. The British promptly imprisoned him. The firebrand refused food for about two weeks and when his health deteriorated, the authorities put him under house arrest to avoid any violent outbursts across the country.

On 17 January 1941, Subhas Bose slipped out of his house into a waiting car. Disguised as a Muslim religious teacher, he managed to reach Peshawar. From there he went to Italy, Germany and Russia to seek help for his cause of freeing India but apparently without success. He went to Singapore and, when the opportune moment arrived, he organized the INA or Indian National Army (Azad Hind Fauj) and led it into battle against the British Empire in India. It had a separate women's unit called Rani of Jhansi Regiment, a never-before-attempted idea in Asia. He displayed a rare genius for organization, strategy and tactics. His eye for detail, sincerity of purpose, passionate faith and burning love for his motherland are perhaps unmatched even today.

Unfortunately, the defeat of Japan and Germany in World War II forced the INA to retreat before it could achieve its objective. Subhas was reportedly killed in a plane crash in August 1945, but many believe that he survived. No information about him is available after that.

The heroic leader wrote his unfinished autobiography, *An Indian Pilgrim*, while recuperating in Bad Gastein, Austria, in 1933. There, he met his Austrian secretary Emilie Schenkl whom he married in 1937. The couple had a daughter, Anita, who is now a professor of economics at the University of Augsburg.

Netaji's immortal words—'Give me blood and I shall give you freedom!'—still echo in our hearts and his heroism is celebrated in literature and in cinematic productions.

Nritya Mayuri

Name: Sudha Chandran
Birth Date: 21 September 1964
Place: Madras, Tamil Nadu

When the famous dance school Kala Sadan refused admission to this five-year-old prodigy, her doting father earnestly requested the teachers to assess her dancing skills. He sincerely believed that she was a gifted artist and wanted to channelize her talent rightly and tap her potential to the fullest. He finally persuaded the principal to allow the girl to perform just once. The principal was stunned.

Sudha Chandran became one of the youngest students of Kala Sadan. She first performed on stage when she was just eight years old. She became an acclaimed dancer during her teens and delivered over seventy-five stage performances, a feat that most dancers during her time could only dream of.

But destiny had other plans for her. In 1981, while travelling by bus to a temple, she met with a serious accident that severely injured her right leg. A few days later, due to a medical lapse, her injured leg developed gangrene and had to be immediately amputated to save her life.

This unexpected turn of events plunged the passionate dancer into depression. Sleepless, restless and painful nights frustrated her. It was one of the most challenging phases of her life as she was in darkness about her future as a dancer. After a while, Sudha slowly started walking with crutches and a wooden leg, and concentrated completely on academics to keep herself busy.

Six months later, Sudha's father began exploring the various possibilities of reviving his daughter's dance career. He took her to Dr P.K. Sethi, a specialist in artificial limbs, and explained her achievements and dreams to him. Dr Sethi motivated Sudha and said that with patience and perseverance, she should be able to dance like she had done before. This reassurance helped her bounce back, as she felt a ray of hope once again.

It was a huge challenge for Dr Sethi to restore the dancer in Sudha. He got her an artificial leg made of aluminium that could rotate easily. This marked the beginning of another struggle. The first challenge was for Sudha to get used to her new leg. Dancing was not at all easy; indeed, it was excruciatingly painful as the external attachment was continuously adapted to accommodate her movements. Every time she bled, her hopes of recovery came crashing. Dr Sethi was so impressed with Sudha's willpower that he keenly observed her dance style and soon designed another leg for her. Further agony followed as Sudha adapted anew to this modified leg.

Three years after the disastrous accident, Sudha got her first opportunity to perform on stage again. She was filled with apprehension. However, once she began performing, she stunned her audience. She received appreciation from many reputed dancers. She captured the attention of the media and shot into stardom overnight.

This inspirational comeback inspired a famous Telugu film called *Mayuri*, in which Sudha played the lead role. Her splendid portrayal of the protagonist was appreciated by critics and she was awarded the 1986 Special Jury Award at the National Film Awards. The film was remade in Hindi as *Nache Mayuri* and received international recognition. This catalysed her brief career in films. She has also enjoyed a stint on television.

Sudha received compensation for the accident after fifteen long years of struggle. Though justice was delayed in her case, it was at least not denied.

This dynamic personality has come a long way now, emphatically leaving her disability behind. Not only has she performed in various countries but she has also enjoyed popularity as an actress, and set up her dance academy in Mumbai.

Sudha Chandran inspires people to dare to rewrite destiny.

A Devoted Environmentalist

Name: Sunderlal Bahuguna
Birth Date: 9 January 1927
Place: Tehri, Uttarakhand

In the early 1980s, the intrepid ecological activist Sunderlal Bahuguna undertook a mammoth 5,000-km trek through Himalayan territory, moving from village to village and eventually meeting then Prime Minister Indira Gandhi. Bahuguna's purpose was clear—to spread awareness and gather support for the Chipko Movement, a non-violent mission to stall deforestation in the Himalayas.

Chipko literally means 'to embrace' in Hindi. The movement involved locals, especially women in rural Himalayan regions, in the prevention of tree felling. Local Chipko activists would hug the trees and challenge government workers to chop them down. The movement empowered the locals and encouraged them to take the responsibility to protect trees in their regions. It gathered much publicity and made the common man think about the ecological hazards of deforestation.

Bahuguna's discussion with Indira Gandhi met with some success. It resulted in the Parliament passing a legislation to ban the felling of trees in some areas. Given his extraordinary leadership and unwavering dedication which made the campaign a household name, Bahuguna became synonymous with the Chipko Movement.

However, the footprints of Bahuguna's activism actually stretch far beyond the movement. He has also worked extensively for the rights of women, the poor, the underprivileged, and the oppressed. He is known for his role in mobilizing Himalayan women to combat the alcoholism that was destroying their menfolk and, in turn, their families.

Bahuguna also led the movement against the building of the Tehri Dam, in the foothills of the Himalayas. When the idea of the Tehri Dam first originated, it was intended to collect and divert water from the Ganges—which flows from a glacier in the Himalayas—to boost water and power supply in the urban region of Delhi. Bahuguna protested vehemently, as he felt that by building the dam the government would tamper with the natural resources of the Himalayas and its people. He highlighted the ecological damage that the dam would cause in the region as well as the trauma of displacement that the locals would have to undergo.

The Tehri dam site stands on the Bhagirathi River. Bahuguna, himself a native of Tehri, made the bank of the Bhagirathi his home during his nineteen-year battle against the building of the dam. In the end, the government had its way and the dam was constructed. The town of Tehri was submerged. Bahuguna and his wife Vimla were sent to another home elsewhere. Many other locals too were evacuated and rehabilitated. A dejected Bahuguna told a journalist, 'Those who swim against the current are always alone. For people like me there are only four things in store: ridicule, neglect, isolation and insult.' However, he also said that he would continue to fight to protect the Himalayas.

Bahuguna is seen as a Gandhian, owing to the non-violent means of protest and resistance he uses. At times, he resorted to hunger strikes for his causes. 'Ecology is permanent economy', was his popular slogan during the Chipko Movement.

Bahuguna's philosophy is based on three As: Austerity (consume less), Alternatives (every problem has a solution and it is close to you), and Afforestation (tree farming will solve many problems).

Bahuguna was awarded the Right Livelihood Award a prestigious award also known as the 'Alternative Nobel Prize'in 1987 and the Padma Vibhushan, India's second highest civilian award, in 2009. He is deeply respected for igniting a grass roots movement to protect India's environment.

The Telecom Moghul

Name: Sunil Mittal
Birth Date: 23 October 1957
Place: Ludhiana, Punjab

This successful first-generation entrepreneur, who hailed from a middle-class family of three children, dared to dream, had a vision and went on to become a billionaire. Strongly supported by his father, Sat Paul, a former member of Parliament, Sunil pursued his dreams after his graduation. Though he knew at the outset that the journey was not going to be easy, he found that the practical difficulties he ultimately faced were much more than what he had imagined.

Sunil Mittal borrowed 20,000 rupees from his father and started trading bicycle spares and hosiery yarn. Though the proceeds were initially low, hope never faded for this dynamic young man. Due to his meagre profits, he was often forced to travel by hitch-hiking on the back of trucks or, when he could afford it, by train. He had to invest sixteen to eighteen hours every day and stay in small lodges while trying to build his fortune.

In 1980, he set up Bharti Overseas Trading Corporation along with his brothers and started importing portable generator sets. This was a great business opportunity and the company became one of the largest importers in India. Three years later, the government imposed a ban on imported gen-sets and Sunil was out of business overnight!

Another business opportunity knocked when he noticed the usage of push-button phones in Taiwan. At that time, India was using rotary dials without speed dial and redial facilities. Mittal saw huge potential in the telecommunications business and started Bharti Telecom Ltd to manufacture fax machines, answering machines as well as push-button telephones under the brand named Beetel.

In 1992, he started the brand Airtel after winning a bid to launch mobile services in India. The same year, his supportive father passed away.

Airtel gradually grew into one of the most competitive service providers due its customer-friendly services. It rapidly crossed the two-billion customer mark after successfully bringing down the national and international mobile rates via Indiaone. The company then entered into a joint venture with Singapore Telecom International for a 650-million-dollar submarine cable project, the country's first ever undersea cable link connecting Chennai and Singapore.

Mittal's Bharti Enterprises soon became one of the leading players in India's private telecom sector. Ranked as the fifth largest wireless service provider, it employs thousands of people all over the world. Sunil has tied up successfully with Walmart and started many retail stores in India. He also created Bharti Comtel along with reputed executives from the mobile industry, to provide human resource services.

Sunil considers himself quite lucky to have a very supportive family that includes his wife Nyna and his three children. His relationship with his brothers is quite strong and he still continues his ventures with them. According to him, however, business pressures have deprived him of most of his hobbies like sky-gliding, flying planes or even playing tennis or golf.

For his contributions, Mittal has been honoured with several awards. He was chosen as one of the top entrepreneurs in the world for 2000 and among 'Stars of Asia' by *Business Week*. He received the IT Man of the Year Award in 2002 from *Dataquest*. In 2005, *Fortune* chose him as the Asia Businessman of the Year. He was awarded the Padma Bhushan in 2007. Mittal still believes that business ventures are ongoing processes and constantly strives to provide world-class services across all countries through his enterprises.

Through his phenomenal philanthropic activities, Mittal has proved to be a socially responsible individual. In fact, he is rated as one of the top twenty-five philanthropists in the world due to his wide range of initiatives under the Bharti Foundation that strives to promote education in India. Bharti Foundation has funded over fifty schools in Madhya Pradesh and also undertaken to train teachers and set up libraries in nearby areas. It has also donated 200 million rupees to the Indian Institute of Technology (Delhi) for building a Bharti School of Technology and Management.

Sunil Mittal is an inspiration to the young generation. His career and personality proves that by chasing one's dreams and exploring unexplored avenues, one can make a difference to the whole world.

Prince of the Himalayas

Name: Tenzing Norgay
Birth Date: May 1914
Place: Khumbu, Nepal
Died: 9 May 1986
Place: Darjeeling, West Bengal

During the 1950s, climbing Mount Everest was a huge challenge for mountaineering enthusiasts due to the extreme weather conditions. Some of them even lost their lives during the dangerous expedition throwing up a big question as to whether the peak was reachable at all!

But two men, a humble Nepalese Sherpa from Darjeeling and a beekeeper from New Zealand, successfully fought the rough terrain and bad weather outbreaks and ultimately reached the peak. They were none other than Tenzing Norgay and Edmund Hillary.

Tenzing and Edmund successfully reached the summit situated at an altitude of about 29,000 ft. on May 29, 1953. Tenzing stuck an ice axe into Mount

Everest with the flags of India, Nepal, the UK and the UN fluttering from it. This was Tenzing's seventh attempt to climb Everest. The courageous feat of these men electrified the world and they became legends overnight, creating a permanent niche for themselves in record books.

Tenzing hailed from a poor peasant family of thirteen children. His birth name was Namgyal Wangdi and he changed to his current name on the advice of a lama. Tenzing is a common name in the Tibetan region. It means 'equilibrium in all its essence' or alternatively, 'keeper of Buddha's teachings'.

Surprisingly, Tenzing did not know his exact date of birth! Based on the weather and crop conditions during his birth, he claimed that he must have been born during the later part of May. When he succeeded in his mission on 29 May he became a celebrity overnight and chose the same date to be his birth date!

Young Tenzing ran away twice from Kathmandu and settled in the Sherpa community in Darjeeling. He initially worked as a trekking porter and later, assisted on mountaineering expeditions. Finally he went on to become a global ambassador of the Sherpa community. He has been named by *Time* magazine as one of the 100 most influential people of the 20th century.

Though Tenzing spoke seven languages, he did not learn to write any of them. However, he dictated and published books narrating his experiences at the Himalayan Frontiers.

The feat of Tenzing and Edmund not only brought fame but also raked up many challenging controversies. Since Tenzing was born in Nepal and brought up in India, each of the countries wanted to declare him as their citizen. He was also often posed the question by interviewers regarding who had reached the peak first. For many years, Tenzing said that it had been a combined team effort. However, several years later, he went on record saying that Edmund had stepped on the summit first.

Tenzing shielded himself from the limelight and politics focusing on his love for climbing and standing up for the Sherpa community. The Sherpas still worship him as he brought the community to the global charts. And this is what the legend himself says.' It has been a long road. . . From a mountain coolie, a bearer of loads, to a wearer of a coat with rows of medals who is carried about in planes and worries about income tax.'

In 1953, Tenzing received the George Medal from Elizabeth II. King Tribhuvan of Nepal also presented him with the Order of the Star of Nepal. In 1959, the Government of India awarded him the Padma Bhushan. Tenzing also received several other decorations through his career. In January 2008, Lukla Airport was renamed Tenzing-Hillary Airport in honour of the pair and their achievement.

Tenzing went on to establish the first mountaineering institute at Darjeeling in order to nurture thousands other upcoming Tenzings. He continued this effort till his last days and passed on valuable knowledge to the younger generation. He started Tenzing Norgay Adventures, a company that conducts trekking tours to the Himalayas. Jamling Norgay, his son, currently manages this venture. Jamling has himself also scaled the summit, an adventure which he later documented in the book entitled *Touching My Father's Soul*.

Creator of a Masterpiece

Name: Thiruvalluvar
Period: Between 1st century BC and 6th century AD

'Generous grants, compassion, righteous rule and succour to the downtrodden are the hallmarks of good governance'—these words by the famous Tamil poet Thiruvalluvar, written over 2,000 years ago, were quoted as recently as 2008 by India's then finance minister P. Chidambaram in the Lok Sabha. Indeed, much of Thiruvalluvar's writings have a timeless quality that keeps them and him relevant even in this day and age.

Thiruvalluvar, also known as Valluvar, is best known for his iconic work, *Thirukkural,* comprising over 1,000 Tamil couplets on the importance of ethics in various aspects of life. It is one of the most celebrated and revered pieces of Tamil literature. The exact period of its composition is not known; scholars estimate that it was produced before the 4th century AD.

There is very little information available about Thiruvalluvar, apart from the fact that he wrote *Thirukkural*. The dates and places of his birth and death and other details of his life are limited to ambiguous estimates. Some believe that he was born in Mylapore and established himself as a writer in the Pandya court in Madurai. Others believe that he was a weaver who led an extremely austere life. There is no clear picture regarding his faith. In fact, the Kanyakumari Historical and Cultural Research Centre has recently suggested that Valluvar was a king who ruled Valluvanadu in the hilly tracts of Kanyakumari in Tamil Nadu.

Those who have read *Thirukkural*, however, say that it has been written with a secular perspective. The material it contains does not idealize any particular religion or god; it is of relevance to a cross section of people, irrespective of country, community and class. This is one of the reasons that it has been translated into over sixty languages. It is referred to as 'the book that never lies'.

One of the few facts that are known about Thiruvalluvar's life is that he married Vasuki, who was exceptionally devoted to him. Thiruvalluvar is said to have shown through his own way of life that one does not need to renounce the family structure and become a hermit to lead a pure, simple, spiritual existence. In fact, the final section of *Thirukkural* speaks of the love between man and woman. The first section relates to 'Virtues' while the second relates to 'Wealth'.

One can gauge from Thiruvalluvar's writing that he was a philosopher and political scientist, besides being a creative person. By expressing his practical, insightful and revolutionary thoughts in *Thirukkural*, he has had a lasting influence on Indian life and culture.

Here are some oft-quoted lines from *Thirukkural*:

- Adversity is nothing sinful,
  But laziness is a disgrace
- Wine cheers only when it is quaffed,
  But love intoxicates at mere sight

The government of Tamil Nadu celebrates 15 January as Thiruvalluvar Day as part of the Pongal celebrations.

The Tiger of Mysore

Name: Tipu Sultan
Birth Date: 20 November 1750
Place: Devanahalli (now Karnataka)
Death Date: 4 May 1799
Place: Seringapatam (now Karnataka)

The year was 1799. The fourth and last Anglo-Mysore war was being fought. Tipu Sultan, the ruler of Mysore, had been betrayed by some of his own men. They had secretly allowed the opposing British-led army an easy entry into Tipu's otherwise impenetrable fort. Tipu was having lunch inside the fort when he got to know of the attack and the treachery of his own men.

Much time had been lost. Chances of his victory were slim. He had two alternatives—one was to protect himself and his family by escaping through the secret exits; the other was to surrender and sign a treaty with the British.

Tipu, also known as the 'Tiger of Mysore', was never one to take the easy way out. 'One day's life of a lion is preferable to hundred years of a jackal', he would say.

Tipu rushed into battle and chose to lead from the front and fight it out till the end. He died on the battlefield, trying to defend his kingdom. People who witnessed his last rites have said that a thunderstorm took place around the time of his burial, adding a pall of gloom that bore testimony to the death of an extraordinary ruler.

Tipu was the son of Hyder Ali, an officer in the Mysore army who rose through the ranks to become the ruler of Mysore. Hyder Ali was illiterate, all the more reason why he gave his son the best education. Tipu was fluent in many languages including Urdu, Kannada, Arabic and Persian. He was also adept at military warfare and political affairs. From a very young age, he began to accompany and support his father in various battles. It is even said that Tipu played a vital role in many of his father's victories.

Tipu became the ruler of Mysore after his father's death in 1782. He was an able administrator and a mighty warrior. He protected his kingdom from the Marathas and the Nizams as well as the British. His victories in the first two Anglo-Mysore wars left the British rattled. Tipu is considered to be one of the most daunting obstacles that the British faced in their conquest of India. He often used his diplomatic ties with the French to tackle his rivals.

Under Tipu's reign, Mysore flourished. Apart from being a competent ruler and valiant soldier, he was also a scholar and poet. Though a Muslim himself, he efficiently governed this kingdom, made up of mostly Hindu subjects. Huge advances were made in agriculture, industry and trade during his reign. He built dams, roads and ports and traded with countries like France, Turkey and Iran. Tipu is credited with encouraging many inventions and innovations in artillery design, and is said to be the brain behind the first war rocket ever used. He is said to have started new coinage, calendars, and a new system of weights and measures. Bangalore's famous botanical garden Lal Bagh, the construction of which was started by Hyder Ali, was completed by Tipu.

Tipu's glorious reign suffered a setback in the third Anglo-Mysore war in which he lost half his kingdom. The fourth Anglo-Mysore war, as mentioned before, claimed his life. Tipu, however, has remained in the minds of people for his legendary bravery, his skill as a warrior and military strategist, his defiance of the British and his creative bent of mind.

His multifaceted personality continues to evoke awe and admiration among many.

Iron Man of India

Name: Vallabhbhai Jhaverbhai Patel
Birth Date: 31 October 1875
Place: Nadiad, Gujarat, British India
Death Date: 15 December 1950
Place: Bombay, Maharashtra

In 1909, lawyer Vallabhbhai Patel was cross-examining a witness in court when he received a note informing him of his wife Jhaverba's demise. Patel is said to have put the note in his pocket after reading, and resumed his questioning. Only when proceedings ended for the day did he react to his bereavement. This is one of the many instances that depict his stoic nature. This trait, along with the fact that he was a man of great determination, earned him the epithet 'Iron Man of India'.

Patel was born in a small village of Gujarat but, from a very young age, harboured dreams of training as a barrister in England. With this aim in mind, he studied law in India and started practising to make enough money to fund his studies abroad. Soon, he had earned himself not only a law degree but also a reputation as a highly competent lawyer. At this point, however, he learnt that his brother Vithalbhai also wanted to study abroad. Immediately, he decided to use his savings to send his brother to study in England, instead of going himself.

However, true to his character, he did not give up on his dreams. He had merely postponed his own plans to help his brother. A few years later, at the age of thirty-six, he finally went to England and enrolled to study law. He finished the course and returned to India to become a very successful barrister in Ahmedabad.

During his stint in England, Patel acquired many English mannerisms, such as wearing suits and playing bridge. These remained a part of his life even after his return to India. He was making a lot of money as a barrister and the thought of pursuing a political career was far from his mind.

However, his life took a turn when he happened to find inspiration in Gandhiji and became actively involved in India's freedom movement. Patel had a talent for mobilizing the masses. He became particularly well known after leading the peasants' revolt in Kheda, Gujarat. Along with his children, Manibehn and Dahyabhai, he took to wearing khadi. He also supported Gandhi extensively during the Swadeshi, Non-cooperation, Civil Disobedience and Quit India movements and a host of other activities that led to India's freedom.

Patel was imprisoned more than once during the freedom movement. His close bond with Gandhiji grew more intense when they were both imprisoned at Yerwada Jail in Pune in 1932. Patel was a trusted aide of the Mahatma right up to the latter's death.

When India gained independence in 1947, Patel became the country's first deputy prime minister, in charge of home affairs, information and broadcasting. One of Patel's greatest achievements is that he accomplished the Herculean task of convincing most princely state rulers to accede their kingdoms in order to form a consolidated India.

Posthumously awarded the Bharat Ratna in 1991, Vallabhbhai Patel, often addressed as Sardarji, remains an icon of brilliance, daring, humility, and patriotism.

The Milkman of India

Name: Verghese Kurien
Birth Date: 26 November 1921
Place: Calicut (now Kozhikode), Kerala

An international board meeting was under way. Officials were discussing ways to improve milk production. They refused to accept India's expertise in this field. In protest, an Indian engineer stormed out of the board room. Smarting at the insult, he later proved India's immense potential by transforming the modest Anand company into Amul, one of the most influential and largest food brands of the world.

Today, more than twenty lakh citizens across 10,000 villages in India sell milk worth about five crore rupees everyday and enjoy economic independence thanks to the vision of a dynamic, self-assured engineer who laid the foundation of arguably the most successful cooperative movement in our country. Appropriately, his memoir is entitled *I Too Had a Dream*.

This brilliant engineer returned to India after studying mechanical engineering at Michigan State University. He worked briefly for the government, as a dairy engineer. In 1949, he decided to resign, so disgusted was he with the shabbily run dairy institute called Anand. However, certain unavoidable circumstances that forced him to stay on in the same company transformed his life. He took the company to such heights that he earned the credit of being the father of India's 'White Revolution'.

Fondly called Doodhwalla ('milkman') by the farmers, Dr Verghese Kurien transformed India from being the lowest per capita consumer of milk to one of the largest milk-producing countries in the world. He built an economically democratic model where farmers were encouraged to become rightfully independent. Thus was born one of the largest and most popular dairy cooperative movements in the world.

Dr Kurien believed that, in addition to tapping the right market, the high potential of the farmers needed to be streamlined and managed. He prodded them to dream, empowered them and urged them to manage their own enterprises to maximize profits.

In times when most farmers owned buffaloes but cow's milk was considered to be the primary milk source, Dr Kurien showed them how to produce condensed milk, baby foods and milk powder using buffalo milk thus opening up a whole new opportunity for profitable business. In addition, his unique experiments with dairy milk booths revolutionized traditional methods of selling milk. He also created innovative approaches by selling other food products in the market. Through his dedicated efforts, the Amul brand became a household name.

Because of his staunch faith in the idea, the Amul pattern became quite successful and created immense growth for both producers and consumers. It was replicated across the nation; currently, more than 175 centres of Amul exist across India.

Dr Kurien struggled against the bureaucracy during his unique experiments. Nonetheless, he never failed to acknowledge the role of those politicians and bureaucrats who helped him achieve his vision. Though his openness and honesty was often not appreciated, few could challenge his integrity and ethics. According to him, the opportunity of creating such a huge revolution was provided by Tribhuvandas Patel during the 1940s. Dr Kurien acknowledges the integrity and patriotism of this politician even today.

Kurien's clarity of vision and the confidence to share it with people at different levels and cadres made him realize his passion and create an impact on all strata of society. His lateral thinking and risk-taking ability coupled with innovative solutions and true belief in his ideas earned him respect all over the world. He has been awarded honours like the Padma Bhushan, Padma Shri, World Food Prize and Ramon Magsaysay Award.

In his eighties now, the inspirational Dr Kurien, with his sparkling eyes and agile brain, has proved that age is really not a limiting factor in order to create a wonderful world.

Father of India's Space Programme

Name: Vikram Sarabhai
Birth Date: 12 August 1919
Place: Ahmedabad, India
Death Date: 31 December 1971
Place: Kovalam, Kerala

This extraordinary scientist was also a successful industrialist, innovator and visionary. He was the pioneer of remote sensing and broadcasting satellites in India. He established many reputed institutions and also steered the Atomic Energy Commission as its chairman.

Vikram Sarabhai hailed from an affluent Jain family of eight children. He received Montessori education, quite a rare phenomenon in those times. Sarabhai was influenced by great Indian personalities who often stayed with his family in Ahmedabad. After his college education at Cambridge, he joined Indian Institute of Science as a research scholar under Sir C.V. Raman.

Sarabhai used science and technology as levers to chart out an illustrious career. He visualized interplanetary and solar physics as an emerging area of research. One of his most significant ventures was the Indian programme for the International Geo-physical Year (1957–58). India's first rocket launching station, Thumba Equatorial Rocket Launching Station [TERLS], was set up by Sarabhai with immense support from Homi Bhabha. After launching Sputnik I and gaining international recognition at the UN General Assembly, Sarabhai successfully convinced the government of the need to start an Indian space programme and established the Indian Space Research Organization (ISRO). Following the tragic death of Homi Bhabha in an air crash, Sarabhai was appointed chairman of the Atomic Energy Commission.

His dialogue with NASA resulted in the establishment of the Satellite Instructional Television Experiment (SITE). This initiative aimed to provide technical experience to India in the field of satellite communications and to educate the people of the country through satellite broadcasting. Sarabhai initiated a satellite fabrication project, which led to the development of Aryabhata, India's first satellite, which was launched after his death.

Sarabhai was a planner, a policymaker, and R&D manager of many areas of science and technology. His research initiatives led to the establishment of atomic power stations. Sarabhai motivated budding scientists, gauged their strengths and went to great lengths to tap their potential to the fullest. He systemically guided them to follow their dreams. He believed that scientists should foster creativity, use their expertise to overcome environmental constraints, and apply their knowledge in diverse areas to effect desirable socio-environmental change. He also emphasized that scientists should be involved in policymaking and administration and urged society to honour their tireless work. Along with his colleagues, he published his findings in Indian and international journals.

Sarabhai wanted science to reach the common man. He harnessed the potential of space science and applied it to fields like education, communication, meteorology and remote sensing. He established various programmes and institutions under his leadership in different domains like pharmaceuticals, textiles and electronics.

The Vikram A. Sarabhai Community Science Centre, Ahmedabad, set up in the 1960s, works to popularize the fields of mathematics and science. Sarabhai set up the first electronic data processing and operations research group for the benefit of the pharmaceuticals industry. The Vikram Sarabhai Space Centre, Thiruvanthapuram, Kerala works to develop satellite launch vehicles and carries out active research in aeronautics and avionics. The Vikram Sarabhai Library at Ahmedabad holds a priceless collection of books, research journals, and white papers on various advances in R&D.

Other organizations established by this legend include the Indian Institute of Management in Ahmedabad,

Ahmedabad Textiles Industrial Research Association, Centre for Environmental Planning and Technology and Blind Men Association. He was also instrumental in setting up the Physical Research Laboratory along with meteorologist K.R. Ramanathan.

Deeply interested in sports, architecture, music and painting, Sarabhai was a thoroughly affable and approachable gentleman. He respected his fellow men, irrespective of his social status.

Sarabhai married Mrinalini Swaminathan in 1942. They have two children, Mallika and Karthikeya. An acclaimed dancer, Mrinalini is also the recipient of the prestigious Padma Bhushan. Together, they founded Darpana Academy of Performing Arts in Ahmedabad.

Sarabhai faced great stress during his last years due to a heavy workload and excessive travelling. This affected his health and he succumbed to heart attack in his sleep.

Sarabhai received the Padma Bhushan and the Shanti Swarup Bhatnagar Medal. The Padma Vibhushan was awarded to him posthumously. Sarabhai gave India a global standing in space research and will always be remembered for his priceless contribution to the Indian space programme.

A Very Suitable Man

Name: Vikram Seth
Birth Date: 20 June 1952
Place: Calcutta, West Bengal

In 1981, Vikram Seth hitch-hiked all the way from China to India via Tibet. During his journey he kept a journal, the contents of which were later published as a travelogue, *From Heaven Lake: Travels Through Sinkiang and Tibet.* This work won him the Thomas Cook Travel Book Award in 1983.

Travel writing is just one of the things that Seth does. He is equally adept at writing novels, poetry, children's books and non-fiction. He is best known for his mammoth novel *A Suitable Boy,* which won worldwide acclaim despite its considerable length.

Seth's father Prem Seth worked with the shoe company Bata. When his job required him to move to London, he took his wife Leila and Vikram along. There, Leila studied law while she was expecting her younger son. She went on to become the first woman judge at Delhi High Court and then India's first woman chief justice.

When the family returned to India, Vikram Seth was sent to study at boarding schools in Dehradun, first Welham Boys' School and later Doon School. In later years, he recalled how he was never very popular in school and was often bullied at Doon due to his poor height, his love for reading and studies and his lack of interest in sports. Seth went on to study at Oxford and Stanford universities, majoring in economics. Eventually, he drifted into writing.

At first, he dabbled in poetry. Then came his travelogue. *The Golden Gate* (1986) was his next major work. A novel written in verse, it is supposed to have stemmed from Seth's life as a student at Stanford. It won rave reviews. Then came *A Suitable Boy*, reflecting many elements from Seth's own life and that of his family. The novel also reflected the course that India as a nation took just after Independence. Seth did a lot of research on India, and the book took him six years to write. Speaking of the book's accuracy in detailing the socio-cultural and political landscape of the time, another renowned writer, Khushwant Singh, has remarked: 'I lived through that period and I couldn't find a flaw. It really is an authentic picture of Nehru's India.' Seth is currently writing the sequel to this novel, *A Suitable Girl*.

Seth didn't write a novel for many years after *A Suitable Boy* but when he finally did, it was called *An Equal Music*. A love story featuring musicians, it has won many admirers for the excellent manner in which it depicts the psychology of musicians. The next well known work of Seth was *Two Lives*, a non-fictional memoir based on his great-uncle Shanti Behari Seth and his German wife Henny Caro. In 2011, he published *The Rivered Earth*, four libretti set to music. Seth has also written for children. *Beastly Tales from Here and There* is his collection of fables from across the world.

Despite his small frame, Seth stands tall in the literary world. He has won the Commonwealth Writers Prize and received the Padma Shri.

The writer divides his time between his home in England and his parents' home in Delhi. A little known fact is that he is fluent in numerous languages, including German, French and Mandarin, apart from Hindi and English.

The Grandmaster

Name: Viswanathan Anand
Birth Date: 11 December 1969
Place: Mayiladuthurai, Tamil Nadu

This whiz kid was all of six years when he started playing chess with his mother. She played a great role in shaping his potential to its maximum and helping him become the youngest Indian Grandmaster (1987) and a world champion at a time when chess was a game dominated by the Russians.

Viswanathan Anand's rise into the limelight was meteoric with a string of successes at national and international chess championships. He was awarded the Padma Shri when he was just eighteen years old and became the first sportsman to receive the Padma Vibhushan.

Anand's family settled down in Chennai during his formative years. His father held a prestigious position in Indian Railways while his mother was an influential socialite with a passion for chess. Anand was the youngest of three siblings.

Vishy, as his friends call him, gained widespread

acclaim by winning the elite chess tournament Reggio Emilia in Italy at the age of twenty-one. He displayed the rare potential of playing the game at lightning speed and emerging a winner in almost all formats (Tournament, Rapid, Blitz, Blindfold, Knockout, Match).

Anand's fame skyrocketed when he became the only non-Soviet to claim the World Champion title twice. His other notable victories at top international tournaments include the World Cup, Corsica Masters as well as Credit Suisse Masters. He has also won challenging computer-simulated games, proving himself as among the best in the world.

One of the top six players to cross the 2,800 mark of the FIDE ratings, Anand enjoyed his career peak during the 2000s when he came out successful among over 600 chess players in the World Blitz championship and also surpassed the top champions in the Rapid Chess Championship. These feats raised his world ranking to number one for the first time in 2007 and he held this title for the next fifteen months. He has won the World Championships five times and is currently the world chess champion having won against Boris Gelfand in 2012.

Fondly called 'The Tiger of Madras', Anand is the proud recipient of many prestigious civilian honours like Padma Shri, Padma Bhushan and Padma Vibhushan apart from top sporting honours like Rajiv Gandhi Khel Ratna and Arjuna Award.

Anand is married to Aruna and the couple have a son. This commerce degree holder is also interested in music, swimming and reading. He maintains his fitness by practising yoga and brisk walking. Success has only humbled him and he keeps his personal life away from media glare.

This respected world champion is involved in various philanthropic initiatives. He donated a gold medal in 2010 for auctioning to an organization called The Foundation. The proceeds of this auction went into the development of resources for underprivileged children. He is is also an active contributor to the NIIT Mind Champions Academy.

Anand aims to promote the game of chess by presenting innovative formats and taking it to the grass roots, making it accessible and interesting to the common man. In 1998, he came up with his first book, *My Best Games of Chess*.

Anand was a guest of honour at a major chess event held at Gujarat University in 2010, which created a world record by featuring nearly 20,000 chess players. He is on the board of directors of the Olympic Gold Quest, which supports and promotes India's young talent for the Olympics.

During his envious career graph spanning over two decades, Anand's name has become synonymous with chess. This versatile champion has always proved to be ahead of his peers and continues to inspire millions of budding players.

Maker of Music

Name: Zakir Hussain
Birth Date: 9 March 1951
Place: Bombay, Maharashtra

It was a concert of maestros. Legendary tabla player Ustad Allah Rakha was performing with famous sarod player Ustad Ali Akbar Khan. Allah Rakha's six-year-old son sat nearby, close to a spare tabla. Unmindful of the crowd, the child started fidgeting with it. It came to him naturally. On an impulse, in the midst of the concert, Allah Rakha asked him, 'Do you want to play?' The boy eagerly said, 'Yes!' His father simply moved offstage. A great musician, whom the world would cherish in coming years, was introduced to the audience in a most candid manner, without any campaign. Six-year-old Zakir Hussain performed impromptu with Ali Akbar Khan for twenty minutes!

This may have been his first public performance but the tabla was not new to this child. Two days after he was born, instead of whispering the *aazan* (Islamic call to prayers) into his ear, his father played the tabla for him to listen to. Often thereafter, the child sat cushioned in his father's lap while he played the instrument. Soon, pots and pans—indeed anything that he could lay his hands on—became the child's instruments to make music.

At three years of age, his formal training began with his father, who also became his guru. The boy's day would start at 2.30 a.m. and he would play the tabla with his father until 6 a.m.

Recognized as the best percussionist in India, Zakir was born to the family of Allah Rakha who himself was the first musician in a family of farmers. Zakir grew up in Mahim, a modest suburb of Bombay, along with his younger brothers Taufiq Qureshi, Fazal Qureshi and Maral Qureshi, who also became noted percussionists.

Keenly observant, Zakir learnt a lot through his surroundings. Street fairs and festivals in the vicinity of their home made a deep impact on his young mind. He would often perform with other drummers during these festivals. Zakir's father inculcated in him the love and devotion to learn. In complete deference to his father and guru, Zakir has always displayed a yearning to learn more. In one of his many interviews, he said, 'There is no such thing as a great musician or artist. All there is, is a great student because there are always new things to learn.'

He began touring for music concerts before he was twelve. As he grew, he had the privilege of playing alongside Pandit Ravi Shankar, Ustad Alauddin Khan, Ustad Amjad Ali Khan, Pandit Hariprasad Chaurasia, Pandit Shiv Kumar Sharma, Pandit Jasraj and Pandit Birju Maharaj.

He was trained to play in the traditional style of the Punjab gharana but Zakir's quest to learn more led him to create music with artists from South India as well as drummers of international repute. He became one of India's first musicians to experiment with fusion music.

Zakir carried the music of India to the international stage. He recorded albums with many internationally famous musicians like George Harrison, Joe Henderson, Van Morrison, Jack Bruce, and Mickey Hart. In 1975, he formed a music group called Shakti. His debut solo album, *Making Music*, was released in 1987.

In 1988, at the age of thirty-five, Hussain became the youngest percussionist to be awarded the Padma Shri. Two years later, he received the Indo-American Award for helping improve relationships between the US and India. He is also the recipient of the 1999 National Heritage Fellowship.

Planet Drum, an album that he created along with Mickey Hart in 1992, received a Grammy for the Best World Music Album. He also won a Grammy for his collaborative album, *Global Drum Project*, in 2009.

Zakir Hussain is not only a brilliant tabla player but also has strong technical knowledge of sound recording. He constantly encourages newer musicians and also teaches in his father's music school in Mumbai. He has composed the music for several films such *Heat and Dust*, *In Custody* and *Little Buddha*.

The maestro is married to noted Kathak dancer Antonia Minnecola and the couple has two daughters, Anisa and Isabella. Despite his towering achievements, Zakir remains a very humble person. Applause from his colleagues gives him bigger satisfaction than any award. Very modestly, he says: 'I'm just thankful to God for the chances I've been blessed with.'

Truly, Ustad Zakir Hussain is a musician who belongs to the world, though his soul is Indian.